MW01518921

Release Your Stress

and Reclaim Your Life

Joseph G. Langen, Ph.D.

Sliding Otter Publications
www.slidingotter.com

Sliding Otter Publications
5 Franklin Ave.
Le Roy, NY 14482
jlangen@slidingotter.com
2014

Table of Contents

Foreword

The American Psychological Association has been conducting a yearly nationwide survey of stress among Americans. In 2013, seventy-two percent of adults felt that their stress had increased over the past five years. Twenty percent of them felt under extreme stress.

About a third of people feel they are doing a good job managing stress. The top sources of stress are reported as money, work, the economy, family responsibilities family health issues and personal health concerns. Most of these people have difficulty finding good ways to manage stress.

I don't know for sure why you are here or what you expect from me and this book, although I have some ideas. I am sure you have questions about stress in your life or you wouldn't be here. I am glad you stopped by. Stress affects everyone today. It has become a national epidemic. Complaints about it are common and solutions not so easy to come by.

Thank you for trusting me enough to see what I have to say. I will work hard to keep your trust on your way to understanding and managing stress in all aspects of your life. Let me start with a few questions others have asked about stress. Maybe some of them occurred to you when you decided to give my book a try.

- **Why is stress such a big deal for everyone these days?** In Chapter 1, we will visit the controversy over whether we have more or less stress than our ancestors and whether stress is an epidemic. I will share a little about my personal journey with stress. We will also consider dealing with stress as a way to a more peaceful life.

- **What is stress and how can I recognize it?** In Chapter 2, I will consider with you the dictionary definition of stress and early research on stress. You will also learn how to recognize that you are under stress even if it doesn't feel that way.

- **Can stress overtake my life when I am not looking?** In Chapter 3, you will come to understand stress which finds you in your daily life without your invitation. Anything new in your life is somewhat stressful to some degree at least for a while and life is a series of changes.

- **Am I responsible for my stress?** You choose a certain degree of stress with each choice you make in life as you will see in Chapter 4. You might not like stress, but sometimes it comes attached to changes you make in order to better your life. You will see which of your choices come with a stress price tag attached.

- **What does stress do to my body?** Your body has a whole range of responses to stress and an arsenal of ways to combat stress. In Chapter 5 you will learn about the connection between stress and your body and how it reacts to stress.

- **What about my mind?** If you think back to the last time you felt under stress, you will recall your mind working furiously for a solution. In Chapter 6, you will learn more about how stress affects your thinking.

- **How does stress affect my feelings?** Under stress, all sorts of troublesome feelings make themselves painfully known. Learn to understand your feelings and emotions as they relate to stress in Chapter 7.

- **How about my soul?** Lately people have come to realize that their bodies and minds are not the only victims of stress. Making sense of your life, including stress, may well involve finding a spiritual context for it. See how in Chapter 8.

- **Is stress ever a good thing?** Learn how it can save your life. Stress can also help motivate you to accomplish things you might not otherwise attempt. See how to use stress to your benefit in Chapter 9.

- **Can I avoid stress?** You can, but there are healthy and unhealthy ways of doing so. Learn the difference in Chapter 10.

- **If I can't avoid stress, how can I take it on and defeat it?** You already have most of the tools you will need lying around. In Chapter 11, you will learn how to find and use them.

- **Can I change stress into something more useful in my life?** Yes you can. It takes a little imagination and work, but you can do it. Learn how to transform your stress in Chapter 12.

- **Will my life keep getting more stressful in the future?** Not necessarily. It depends on choices you make for yourself and for the world you live in. Learn what they are in Chapter 13.

Okay, those are some general questions people ask about stress. What about you? Maybe you chose this book because you are burdened with a great deal of stress right now. I suggest writing down what you learn about stress and about yourself from time to time as we proceed. For starters, here are a few things you might ask yourself before we begin our journey together:

- **How much stress do I feel right now?** Try rating it on a scale of one to ten with one being completely relaxed and ten being one step from throwing in the towel.

- **How long have I been suffering from my current stress?** Is it something that just happened to you recently or has it been plaguing you for years?

- **What contributes to my stress?** Sometimes your stressors stare you in the face. Sometimes you have to do some digging to uncover them. When you find them, make a list for later.

- **How comfortable am I with my ability to come to terms with my stress?** Do you trust yourself to solve this problem?

- **Have I been here before?** If so, you might remember what you did last time to get out of this mess.

- **Who can I count on to help me in this struggle?** Perhaps you know someone who has faced your same situation. Or you might know someone who is a good listener and is also willing to help.

After this exercise, you should have a little better handle on what you are facing. Knowing what the problem is always helps when you are looking for solutions. Try to be patient with yourself while we seek to understand your stress and look for some answers for you. On with the journey!

Before we get started, I would like to acknowledge support for my writing efforts and this book in particular from Carol Gomborone, Bob Fussell, Beth Cahany and Mary Dougherty. Special thanks to Gerry Lanning for his tireless help polishing my manuscript, above and beyond the call of duty.

Chapter 1- The Stress Landscape

Reality is the leading cause of stress
among those in touch with it.

~Lily Tomlin~

Stress Over the Ages

What does stress feel like in your life? Do people these days suffer more stress than their ancestors? You can idealize the past when life was not so complex and consider earlier centuries as idyllic. You can name all the pressures of modern civilization and feel more beset by stress than those who preceded you by several decades or even centuries. Or you can view your ancestors as at a disadvantage due to the lack of modern conveniences on which we have come to rely.

In the past, people did not worry about stress. Survival and the demands of daily life absorbed most of their energy. They had little time for worry. Yet over the years, fretting about stress seems to have become a national pastime. It is almost a contest to see who is under the most stress.

My Major Stressors

I would like to share with you four major stressors which I have encountered during my life. You might think these would create significant stress for you or perhaps not. I have discovered that one person can be thrown off balance by something which another person might take in stride. Maybe my experiences will bring to mind experiences which have been difficult for you to handle. Yours might be very different from mine.

The first major stressor in my life and the only one I recall from my childhood was my circumcision at age eight. The controversy over circumcision was in full swing when I was born. My father was in Guam in the Navy during World War II. My mother did not want to make the decision by herself, so she put it off.

When I was eight, my parents decided it was time for me to be circumcised. I never got a satisfactory explanation for why this was necessary, either then or later. I have never been comfortable discussing it openly and never asked for an explanation from my parents who are now both deceased.

I was just told it was scheduled. I was left in the hospital the night before surgery and did my best to dodge questions by my roommate about why I was there. I was terrified my whole time in the hospital. The only things I remembered the next day were shots which I had always dreaded and the horrible smell of ether after I was wheeled to the operating room. I woke up in a ward full of children recovering from their own surgeries.

The hardest part of the whole ordeal was returning to school and trying to find a satisfactory explanation for being in the hospital without admitting why. All I could do was hang my head and blush. For years after that, I wondered why the Catholic Church celebrated the circumcision of Jesus on January 1. I eventually learned about its religious significance for Jews. But I was not Jewish. I had no choice about this stressor appearing in my life.

My second major stressor appeared when I was thirteen years old and my grandfather died suddenly. He had lived with a heart condition and took nitroglycerine pills. One day he decided to shovel snow, felt some chest pain and made his way back inside but didn't make it to his pills in time.

He was the kindest person I ever met and he acted as my father for the first few years of my life since my father was off in the Pacific for World War II. At his funeral, our family sat in the parlor sharing stories of my grandfather. Someone asked whether he had ever been angry.

After considerable deliberation and head scratching, My Aunt Helen recalled one time when two of my uncles chased each other through the house while my grandfather sat in his chair with his beer and limburger cheese. On their third pass through the house, my grandfather told them to stop running through the house. They kept running. On the fourth pass he got out of his chair with the intention of stopping them. He realized he would never catch them and sat back down in his chair with his customary laugh.

If I could have chosen one person to be like when I grew up, it would have been my grandfather. His death left a deep hole in my heart, a loss I have never forgotten. This was the first close relative of mine to die that I could remember. I have never found anyone to replace him but still live my life as I imagine he would want me to.

The third stressor I want to share with you was when I was twenty-two. I had spent nine years in a seminary and monastery starting at age thirteen with hours set aside every day to reflect on myself, my relationship with God and how I should live my life. Extended time for reflection allowed me to put stress on the back burner for the most part.

I had a schedule to follow so I did not even need to decide what to do each day. My food, clothing and housing were of no concern to me. I had no need to worry about how to make a living. In some ways this might sound like an ideal world. Why I am not still there is a long story. If you are interested, you can find my account in my memoir, *Young Man of the Cloth.*

The transition back to life in the larger world left me feeling like a fish out of water. I left the monastery and switched from having ample time for reflection to facing pressing questions about where to live, how to survive and what to do about my military draft status which immediately became 1A.

I went from a life in which I had no decisions to make to one for which I was ill prepared. Before I faced many of the stressors I will address in this book, the stress of leaving the only life I had known since I was thirteen descended on me. I made the choice to dive back into an unknown world, not knowing what to expect.

The fourth of my major stressors was my divorce after twenty-nine years of marriage. Mental illness had torn my family apart to the point that marriage was no longer tenable for me. After working for so many years helping others preserve their marriages, I felt embarrassed that I was not able to hold my own together.

I had always seen myself as a man of my word. What about my promise to stay married "until death do you part?" The only way I could make sense of it and live with myself was to realize that my marriage was dead and that we needed to part, or at least I did. This stressor was partly thrust on me and partly my choice.

Stress and My Career

You might wonder whether writing this book caused me stress. Several people have asked me this question. The short answer is no. I find myself living in a world riddled by stress, everyone complaining about how difficult they find life. Well, maybe not everyone, but it sure seems that

3

way. Why is life so stressful? Is it worse now than it ever was? Does stress fall on you like a ton of bricks or do you bring it on yourself?

As a psychologist, I worked with many people over the years, most of whom viewed stress of one sort or another as chief among their concerns. Parents dragged in their children, their families crumbling under stress. Teens considered suicide as a way out. Young adults stewed and fretted over their future. Couples complained of the burdens arriving with their marriages. Older people reeled from the onset of aging, retirement and the changes both required.

Stress seems universal although descending upon us in many different forms. People seeking help do not always admit suffering from stress at first or even recognize it, but they usually discover its impact on their lives before too long once they start talking about their lives in counseling. Most of them do not really care what stress is. They just want it to go away. They want quick answers involving as little disruption to their routines as possible and easy steps toward a less stressful life.

Stress seems like an epidemic. Why? Our culture encourages us to demand everything immediately if not sooner, especially anything that keeps our busy pace of life rolling along as fast as possible. Fast food, next or same day service and turbo speed Internet service have become our birthright claim. Yet, the faster our lives spin, the less time we have to stop and think about what our lives are all about.

Ever stop to think about your pace of life? People these days tend to get caught up in the whirlwind of life in the twenty-first century and keep moving as quickly as possible, seldom looking back to see where they have been or even where they are now.

What You Can Expect From This Book

So, why did I write this book? Dealing with stress is a lifelong undertaking in my opinion. Still learning to cope with stress which arose with each new life experience, I worked for quite a few years helping one individual or family at a time with their particular stress. I found myself listening to the same stories and repeating the same advice over and over.

I came to realize that stress is almost a universal condition of life in modern society. Now that I have retired from my psychology practice, I thought it might be time to share what I have learned over the years for the benefit of more people than I could reach one at a time.

I do not see myself as having the ultimate answers to stress. I think I have learned how to make sense of stress, understand where it comes from and how it affects people as well as what can be done about it. My goal is to help you understand stress and why it is in your life as well as to arm you for your battles with stress. Hopefully you will begin to see them instead as challenges which make you better equipped for the succeeding steps in your life journey.

First we will consider what stress is and how it came to be of importance to psychologists. Along the way, you will see how stress affects your body, mind, emotions and your spirit, or soul if you prefer. We will explore the causes of stress, both those you choose and those dumped on you for one reason or another or sometimes for no particular reason you can see. We will look at what you can do to avoid stress, make your life less stressful and even transform stress into something useful to you.

I invite you to share this journey toward a more peaceful life. I have no quick answers. But I can suggest tools for you to use in understanding and managing your stress. We will also look at choices which increase or decrease your stress. Take a deep breath, relax and let's get started.

But first, let's take a little break from our journey. In my *Sliding Otter Newsletter*, I always end each article with Life Lab Lessons, reflections on what you can learn from your experience and reading. I will end each chapter with a few things for you to think about. Here are some for right now.

Life Lab Lessons

- **When did you first discover stress?** When do you remember first experiencing stress in your life? You may recall feeling lonely, afraid, or maybe angry? Were you one of the lucky ones who had a wonderful childhood? Perhaps you were and can't remember any stress as a child. You might have felt lonely, scared or angry. These feelings all indicate stress.

- **What troubled you most as a child?** I told you about one childhood experience of mine which thoroughly humiliated me. Did anything like that happen to you? Write down what you remember about it.

- **Who helped you deal with past stress?** Were you left to handle your stress by yourself or did someone recognize how you felt, help you to understand what was happening and learn how to get past it. If you had someone help you as a child, I am sure you are grateful to have had him or her in your life.

- **What major trials have you faced as an adult?** List them and think about how they affected you. Have you gotten past them or do they still bother you?

- **Are you burdened by any major stressors right now?** If you are currently struggling with major stressors, they may be hard for you to face calmly right now. We will get to what you can do about them later in the book.

Chapter 2- What Is Stress?

Tension is who you think you should be.
Relaxation is who you are.

~Chinese Proverb~

You probably think you know what stress is. Everybody experiences it from time to time and some people find it a daily companion. You know it when it has you in its grip and how it feels. Putting how you feel into words is a little more difficult. Since it is so much a part of everyday life, you might think psychologists would have developed a way to help make sense of stress and figure out how to manage it. Progress has been made over the years yet stress remains a bit of a mystery.

The Dictionary and Beyond

The word stress is defined in many ways. Stress can refer to the events or circumstances which beset you. It can mean the process in which various parts of your body struggle to cope with an unwanted situation. It can also mean your thoughts and emotions become off kilter after something unexpected happens to you. Perhaps you think of stress as coming at you out of nowhere. Yet you frequently create your own stress whether you realize it or not.

Sometimes you accept it willingly as part of the price you pay to get something you want and sometimes you don't recognize it until it has knocked you for a loop. Did you think the world of stress would be easy to understand? I am afraid it is somewhat complicated. Please bear with me. This chapter is the most technical one in the book. It will be easier going once we get down the road a bit.

Just so you understand where we are headed, I would like to clarify a few terms before we get too far. As you saw, the word stress can mean quite a few things. In this book, I will use the word "stressor" to mean any event or situation which leads to stress in your life. It could be something you or someone else does which leaves you feeling off balance. It could be a mess you were born into or in which you landed as your life progressed. It might also be something you choose or which just lands in your lap.

I will use the word stress to mean your reaction to the stressors you encounter. These reactions include responses of your body to protect you from attack. You can also react with thoughts about your stressors, experience unpleasant emotions or feelings which result from them, and change how you see yourself and your life, what I call the spiritual dimension. We will consider all of these reactions during the course of our journey together through the world of stress.

You might view stress as a feeling of being overwhelmed by pressures in your life beyond your ability to cope with them. Here are some signs of stress:

- You feel anxious, grouchy, isolated or inadequate.

- Your body sends up distress signals such as headaches, an upset stomach or bowel, high blood pressure, trouble sleeping or trouble with your love life.

- You feel out of touch with others, afraid of relationships or wary of commitments of any sort.

- Inside, you feel depressed or nervous.

- You become edgy, overreacting to almost everything.

- You bark at people who don't do what you think they should.

- You get down on yourself when you don't meet your own standards.

- You show a pattern of road rage.

These are signs that you are experiencing stress in your life although they might also appear for other reasons. Many people try to take stress in stride and wait for it to blow over. On occasion this approach works but usually you must rely on stronger measures.

Stress Taken Seriously

Here is the really technical part. The Hungarian endocrinologist Hans Selye brought stress to medical and psychological attention describing it as "the non-specific response of the body to any demand for change." He researched the body's reaction to stress and the body's ability to cope with it.

As an endocrinologist, he became fascinated by the intricate network of chemical messengers circulating in the blood stream. He studied what happens to this messaging system when the body encounters stress and how the messengers work together to return the body to a normal state of equilibrium which he called homeostasis.

Selye saw stress as a response of the body which we will consider further in a later chapter. For now, remember that the body is not the only place you experience stress. Your mind, emotions and soul react as well. We will also consider these dimensions in separate chapters as we go further into our discussion of stress.

Selye did not define the word stressor beyond describing it as anything that produces stress. As we know, he saw stress as the body reacting to a demand for change. That makes sense. Doing something new is harder than doing what you have done all along. Change involves facing the unknown and sailing into uncharted waters. If you want anything to be different in your life, facing change becomes inevitable.

Yet sticking with the same old routine can also become stressful. You might tire of doing the same thing over and over. You can outgrow the results of your old habits and be ready for something new. Sticking with old patterns might seem safer but it has its limitations, especially if new priorities emerge in your life demanding new actions on your part.

What about the demand for change Selye mentioned when he defined stress as "the non-specific response of the body to any demand for change?" Choosing to do something new has its risks and braving the unknown presents an occasion to feel stress. If you are changing by choice, it seems likely that you will feel less stress since you have some control over the direction in which you are headed. If the change is thrust on you, it usually comes with a heavier burden of stress.

Here's an example from my own experience. As I said, I lived in a seminary and monastery for nine years, starting at age thirteen. At the end of the nine years, it became apparent to me that the religious order I joined had chosen a path back toward the eighteenth century when I was expecting a change leading toward the future.

I had been excited about the changes I saw coming for my religious order and for the Catholic Church as a whole. In my opinion, the promised changes felt threatening to the order which wished to retreat into an older and more traditional approach to religious life.

I was faced with a dilemma: I could either keep living in what I saw as outmoded ways or strike out on my own in another direction. At the age of twenty-two, I faced the larger world again after leaving it at age thirteen to enter the seminary. For me that was real stress.

Stress and Its Challenges

While your body struggles to manage stress, your mind also deals with it. Minor stress inconveniences you. Major stress can immobilize you. Yet not all stress is bad. A certain amount sharpens you and helps keep you on your toes. Completely relaxed, you tend to be lackadaisical. This is fine sometimes but not day in and day out.

Recently I read an article about teens in one Florida school district. They lived in a part of the country largely populated by people much older than they were. They did not feel taken seriously by the senior citizens who surrounded them and who received most of Florida's attention. As a result they felt under a great deal of stress. Feeling overwhelmed by life may be based partly on how you live and partly on circumstances in which you find yourself as we shall see.

Psychiatrists and psychologists have studied the mental and emotional effects of stress in addition to the physical strain. In my experience as a psychologist, I don't recall seeing anyone for treatment who did not complain of stress in some fashion. Patients seek treatment when stress overwhelms them and leave treatment when they find a way to manage their stress. This tends to be true for adults and teens as well as for children.

Stress is not an issue just for those people seeking mental health treatment. Physical illness is often caused by stress or made worse by it. Children feel stress in school and sometimes in their friendships. Adults feel stress from parenting challenges, work pressures and financial strain. Illness creates stress for patients as well as for their families. Your relationships with others can produce stress as well.

Understanding stress and where it comes from is more complicated than you might think. And then there is the whole issue of what to do about it. In this book I intend to help you find a way to make sense of stress. You will learn where it comes from, what it does to your body, mind, emotions and soul. You will also learn what to do about it.

Your Stress Window

Maybe this would be a good place to introduce the Johari Window, developed by psychologists Joseph Luft and Harry Ingham, in case you have not heard of it. The window is a way to consider what you and others know about you. I have adapted it to use in considering stress in your life, what you are aware of and what is obvious to others.

Open	Blind
Private	Mystery

The boxes represent what there is to know about a person, you for example. Suppose we concentrate on the stress in your life. The **Open** part includes your stressors which you know about and which are also obvious to others. If your spouse just died, you face major stress obvious to all including you.

The **Blind** part represents stress which others can see in you but you can't. You might start showing a pattern of coming to work late each day, haggard and disheveled, and having trouble concentrating on work or getting assignments done on time. When someone asks if you are okay, you say you are fine and might even believe it. You're not fine and you are the only one who doesn't know it.

The **Private** part is your stress which you know about but others don't. You know where it comes from and how it affects you. Yet when someone asks you what's bothering you they hear that nothing is wrong and you are fine. You might show symptoms of stress but pretend to be okay.

The **Mystery** part is trickier and harder to pin down. It consists of stress which is not obvious to others or to you. So how do you know it exists? Your body knows and so does your mind. Something is wrong but it is not clear what. You most likely need help pinning it down and figuring out what to do about it.

Keeping Secrets from Yourself

This idea sounds a bit odd to me even though I thought it up. How can you keep a secret from yourself? If you did keep it from yourself, how would you know it was a secret? Both good questions. Let's see if we can find some answers.

Maybe it would be easiest to start with secrets you know you have. Take a moment to think about things no one else knows about you. Why are they secrets? Perhaps you did something which shames you. You could have done something illegal and would face consequences if you were discovered. Or maybe you did something which was not illegal but still mortifying for you to recall.

What if you let down a friend whom you could easily have helped, but didn't? You can't think of any good excuse for not rising to the occasion. You would not want anyone to know about it and think ill of you as a consequence. It's even hard for you to think of yourself as doing something like that.

Perhaps someone treated you in a way which deeply embarrassed you. It is not your fault that it happened, but it demeans you. Survivors of sexual abuse often feel this way. You don't know what people would think of you if they knew about it and don't care to find out.

Memories of experiences such as abuse can torture you every time they come to mind. If your recollection of the events and how you reacted to them are troublesome enough, your mind might change a few details or perhaps the whole memory. Freud suggested that it's possible to repress memories. Current research studies are exploring parts of the brain involved in this process. So it does seem possible to keep memories a secret from yourself.

I wonder, though, whether erasing the memory also shuts off the thoughts about yourself because of what happened and the feelings which go along with it. I have met people who have a memory that "something might have happened." They don't know what happened, if anything, and are afraid to find out. They would rather leave things as they are rather than delving into the possibilities. But they remain troubled by the unknown.

If you work hard enough to stop a memory and replace it with other thoughts, you can block a memory. If you are successful, what happened fades into the unknown, even if your feelings about it remain with you. But if you "unlearned" this memory, you can relearn it if and when you are ready.

Maybe now that time has passed, you will be ready to face what happened and settle your feelings about it. Then you can proceed with a clean slate without looking over your shoulder to see what memories might be trying to catch up with you.

A Practical Aside

If you are reading this book because you are hounded by stress and don't know what to do about it, here is a practical suggestion. Don't panic! You have lived with stress this long even though it might not be comfortable. Set aside a period of time during your day just for you with no interruptions.

My friend, John Mangan, a psychologist I worked with many years ago, wrote in his appointment book several times a week "John Alone." I asked him about it and he told me it was time for him to unwind and enjoy his own company for a while. Why should his patients get all his best time? Take "alone time" for yourself and use it to be kind to yourself. Then you will have taken the first step toward getting your stress under control.

Calculating Your Stress

As you have just seen, it is not always easy to know how much stress you carry around with you. Whatever your situation, you become accustomed to it and consider it almost normal after a while, no matter how big a toll it takes on you. Here are a few questions to consider as we start our journey.

You might want to write down the answers to keep them in mind as we move along toward solutions. All of these are signs of stress. This book is designed to help you understand what makes you feel stress, what stress does to you on various levels and what to do about it.

Life Lab Lessons

- Are you frequently unsure of yourself?
- Do you tend to be a pessimist?

- Are you full of pep and energy or do you constantly feel tired?
- Do you usually wake up feeling rested or perhaps feeling restless and worried?
- Do you have a good memory or do you forget what's on your agenda?
- Are you constantly late for appointments?
- Do you feel pressured or rushed to get things done?
- Do you feel like you have too much to do on a daily basis?
- Do you feel burned out?
- Do you battle angry feelings even in small matters?
- Do you have trouble finding time to spend doing what you enjoy?
- Are you patient with others or do you snap at them without understanding why?
- Do you avoid spending time with others?
- Do you feel lonely?
- Do your friends see any of the above as issues for you?

Chapter 3- Stress You Do Not Choose

I try to take one day at a time,
but sometimes several days attack me at once.

~Jennifer Yane~

Now that you have an idea what stress is, where does it come from? Most people want to relieve their stress and eliminate it as soon as soon as they begin to feel its presence Have you ever wondered where your stress comes from? Regardless of what you know about stress and its origin, it's often painful to face. Maybe you would rather not face it at all. But I don't think you want to live with it on a daily basis either.

If you are constantly battling stressful feelings, it's hard to concentrate on what you want to do with your life. It can be very discouraging. Putting out fires without knowing what started them keeps you hopping day after day to keep up with them and there is no end in sight. If you don't know where your stress comes from, how will you know what to do about it?

Let's look at some of the origins of stress. They are different for everyone. Sometimes you battle stress like it's a foreign invader, something totally outside yourself. At other times, you invite stress into your life for various reasons. In this chapter, let's start with stress which sneaks up on you and for which you didn't volunteer.

There it is complicating your life when you least expect it. What are these uninvited stressors? I am sure you can think of some of them. I have not included all of them here, but I will outline some of the more common ones which you might encounter in your life. Take a look.

Your Family

You learned what society expected of you from your family unless life suddenly landed you in a foster or adoptive home or possibly an institution. Switching families midstream in your childhood can be confusing and requires quite a bit of flexibility not common to most children.

Perhaps you parents divorced and you became part of another family when one of them remarried. You now have more than one set of rules to which

15

you must adjust. Making sure this works smoothly requires patience and sensitivity on the part of all concerned.

As a baby you sensed whether you were in a protective environment while still in your mother's womb even though you did not have words for this until you were much older. Your body adapted to your mother's stress level even before birth. After birth, you continued to react by way of your built-in "stress thermometer." I am sure you can tell the difference between a contented baby and one who is insecure.

As you became more aware of your physical environment, you also developed a sense of whether your family was a safe or stressful place to be. It was still just a feeling. As you started to make friends, you compared your family with those of your friends, again for better or worse. By then you could start to reflect on the differences you saw and put them into words.

Based on your experience, you might have come to appreciate your family or wished you had a different one. You probably didn't think of your family shortcomings as creating stress but now you know what it feels like to grow up in a stressful family if indeed you did.

Your Neighborhood

Your neighborhood and town serves as your physical environment now as it did during your childhood. When you were born, did your parents consult you about where you wanted to live? I didn't think so. You had no say in where your family lived when you were born. It's just where you were. As a young child you most likely didn't think much about where you lived either. You just accepted it. What could you have compared it with? As you started attending school, you became aware of how other children lived, for better or worse.

You might have been fortunate enough to live in a peaceful home in a good neighborhood with loving parents. On the other hand you might have been surrounded by noisy, scary arguments and maybe even bullets flying though the walls and windows of your home. This is more than stressful. It's life threatening.

Maybe your neighborhood was safe enough for you to play along the street or at a nearby playground. Or it might have required taking your life in your hands every time you stepped outside.

Whether you realize it or not, where you grew up influenced how you feel about the rest of the world and about yourself for that matter. After all it was your first experience stepping outside of your family environment. Depending on your circumstances, the world might have appeared as a wonderland full of great adventure or it might have seemed like a scary place and one to avoid at all costs.

We Hold These Truths

As a child, your parents explained and showed you what their beliefs and values were. Most likely you adopted them as your own, at least for a while. That's all you knew until you ran across other families and their ways. Sometime during childhood, you started to evaluate what you learned from your parents. Over time you met other children and their families who thought about life in a way different from how your family thought and lived. At some point in the comparison, you started to develop your own standards, evaluating the ways of life you encountered and adopting what made sense for you.

This process lasts a lifetime. You are constantly exposed to new ideas unless you shut them out of your mind and refuse to pay any attention to them. New ideas challenge old ones and then you have choices to make. As I've explained, you often experience stress when faced with change. This can happen at any time in your life although you may not identify it as stress.

All sorts of new ideas arrive by way of your contact with others whether in person, through reading, television, the Internet or other channels of information. Not all of what you experience matches what your parents believed and valued or even what you have come to believe and value. You might discover that what you previously held sacred is not really true or not particularly useful for your life.

Change is stressful. To change, you must give up part of your old, comfortable ways and face unknown and untried ones. If you come from a family which encouraged you to explore new ways of thinking and acting, it might not be quite so much of a challenge. If you come from a more rigid family, your new ideas might be taken as a betrayal of your family traditions. You could be seen as rocking the family boat or even trying to sink it.

Family Issues

Even spouses who weather the stresses of marriage most of the time and work together to face life's challenges eventually come face to face with stressors they never imagined. When a child is born, his or her parents usually have dreams and plans for their child's future, none involving stress. What were yours if you have children?

Some children seem to sail through life with relatively few storms or even typhoons, live up to their parents' expectations and meet their own goals without too much difficulty. Some children are born with birth defects, threatening their very existence and making their survival difficult from the start.

Still other children struggle with intellectual limitations, emotional difficulties or bodily diseases their parents never anticipated. Adapting to their special needs creates its own stress for the whole family.

Parents of a special needs child sometimes blame themselves for their child's struggle regardless of whether or not they contributed to the problem. Even if they had no hand in causing their child's difficulty, they can still feel responsible and guilty for bringing him or her into the world.

They might feel more stress from the situation than their child does. Their child's difficulties might also cause them more stress than if they were afflicted themselves. We will look more closely at guilt a little later.

Physical or mental illness of one family member affects all the other members. I recall a group exercise in which each person had a string running from them to each of the others in the group. Every time one person moved, all the others felt it.

Another exercise consists of tying one end of a string from each family member to other family members representing their various family relationships including parents, children, siblings and spouses. When any of them moved, the effect on all the others with ties became quite clear and dramatic. The more strings, the greater and more complicated the effect on everyone.

Of course you know how your family members are related to each other. Well, maybe not always. I have met several people who discovered later in life that their real mother or father was not the person who raised them.

Others later discovered sisters or brothers whose identity was hidden by their parents because they were given up for adoption. This causes siblings to change their whole idea of who their family is. Needless to say, this can be very difficult to accept and adapt to.

It might not be clear how something happening to one family member affects everyone else. One example is a family I once saw. The younger of two girls suffered from a condition requiring the attention and support of the whole family in order for her to survive. Her older sister felt ignored due to all the attention given to her.

While tending to major difficulties of one child, it is easy to overlook the effect on the other children and put their needs on the back burner at least until they find ways to show that they need attention too.

Sexual Orientation

Young children do not think of themselves as gay or straight. Children of each gender might prefer to play with traditional toys of same gender children or those of the opposite gender.

I remember one seven year old boy who grew up in the heyday of Power Rangers. He always wanted to be the pink power ranger and liked dolls better than trucks. His parents were horrified about his preferences and wanted him insulated against turning out to be gay. I tried to help his parents accept him as he was and for whoever he would be when he grew up.

Most gay adults I have met sensed their gender identity between middle childhood and adolescence, but many did not talk about it with their families or even with their friends. As children become aware of their orientation, they also sense their family's and friends' level of tolerance and acceptance for their emerging sexual orientation.

While some families prove to be loving and accepting of their children despite the news, other families reject their children's "choice" of lifestyle. These children and teens also face fears of rejection by their peers, teachers, coaches and other adults who appear in their lives. It has saddened me to meet gay men and women who feared the consequences of coming out to their parents even well into adulthood.

Suicide attempts and suicidal thoughts plague many gay teens. As they grow a little older, they seek relationships in which their sexual identity is acceptable. Some teens try their best to hide their sexual orientation.

As adults they might even marry a person of the opposite sex or look for sanctuary in the clerical or religious life as a way of trying to hide from their truth. Many finally do come with their sexual orientation in one way or another but usually not without a struggle.

Living in a Troubled World

As a child, you met your relatives, new friends and their families. Most likely you were enrolled in institutional environments such as schools and churches. Churches, schools and other social institutions promote and expect adherence to their rules which might support or conflict with the rules, norms and expectations you learn at home.

If you are like most other people, as you grew into your teen years you began to question everything including what your family, church and school expected or required you to think, feel and believe. As you decided what was important to you, your values might have developed in a way different from the values of the adults around you.

No doubt you have met people whose values conflict with your own. Where do you stand on issues such as gun control, sexual behavior, gay marriage, capital punishment, war, social welfare, government control or hcw people should behave in public? It's not so hard when people agree with you but more difficult when they don't.

How do you react when they don't? You can keep your mouth shut, try to persuade them to accept your views or hear them out and try to respect your differences. In any case you have choices to make, all of which have consequences for your relationships. Let's move away now from family life and look at some other sources of unplanned stress.

Illness

Stress and illness form a two-way street. Any physical or mental illness you encounter leads to stress for you as well as for those who care about you. Stress also serves as a major factor in producing physical and mental illnesses. A little later, we will consider how stress affects your physical and mental health. Right now, let's think about how health problems add to your stress.

Passing encounters with stress might throw you off balance for a bit but usually do not have a lasting effect on your health. Chronic stress is a different story. Take a look at what happens when you are saddled with it:

- Sometimes it's hard to get up in the morning if illness has kept you from sleeping.

- Your responsibilities create a heavier burden on you when you are exhausted.

- Challenges you previously met with ease or perhaps with a little effort may now seem overwhelming.

- Even if you manage to get out of bed, any number of bodily ailments can deter you from your daily routine.

- You wonder how long will you be laid up.

- You have concerns about when you will be able to get back to your normal daily routine.

- You question whether you will ever be the same as you were in the past.

What if you can't continue to pursue your life dreams and have reached a dead end? You can easily become trapped in a series of "what if" worries. You find yourself digging a deeper and deeper hole, imagining there is no way out, a common reaction at first. Yet there is always something you can do, even if the options are not exactly the ones you would like. But we are getting ahead of ourselves. Later in the book, we will look at options for handling stress.

When I had pneumonia, I was laid out flat and couldn't even drag myself to the doctor's office. Fortunately my daughter rose to the occasion. Sound familiar? If not, you have been lucky so far. Most of us don't sail through life without at least some bouts of serious illness and its associated stress.

Terminal Illness

Worst is terminal illness. If you know you only have a limited time to live, you face some major challenges Even if death is not imminent, being out of commission creates its own stress. What about the people who have come to depend on you? What good are you to them now?

No more business as usual. Regardless of what you believe about the afterlife or what you have heard about its possibilities, you have never been down this road before. The unknown looms before you and approaches rapidly.

Even if you have many supportive people around you in your final days and hours, ultimately you face death alone. I have heard people say they do not fear death. But I imagine most of us will face it with at least a little trepidation when the time comes. After all it is another unknown.

The Grip of Mental Illness

Mental illness can also weigh you down with stress, whether it is your own affliction or that of someone close to you. Depression pulls you into a pit similar to the worry pit we just discussed in relation to physical illness. A moderate level of depression leaves you wondering if you will ever be normal again. Deep depression can lead to feelings of hopelessness and even consideration of suicide as a way out.

Anxiety also occurs on several different levels. I am sure you've felt a little tense at times but eventually got over it. Chronic anxiety is a state of constant worry, sometimes over small or insignificant matters. It can also increase to the point where you feel paralyzed and fear everything around you including your own actions or inaction.

You have most likely heard the many terms for various kinds of phobia focused on everything from elevators to going outside your front door. At the extreme, generalized anxiety disorder leaves you with tension and worry wracking your mind most of the time and you are not easily able to identify what makes you feel anxious in the first place.

Bipolar disorder takes you on a roller coaster of ups and downs, sometimes between a normal mood and serious depression, sometimes between normal and manic states in which your mind races wildly and you act unpredictably and sometimes between depression and mania. Imagine the stress of not knowing what to expect of your mind and emotions each day when you wake up.

Schizophrenia takes you on another wild ride where you can't trust your perceptions. Sometimes it prevents you from knowing what is real and what is imagined. In addition to making it difficult to live with yourself, it also makes it hard for others to be around you, not knowing what to expect from you. We will consider mental illness in more detail in Chapter 6.

Loss of Loved Ones

Although not in your plans, those you love sometimes die before you do. The longer you live, the more likely it is that you will face this particular stressor. Sometimes you have a chance to prepare for losing a loved one. The loss can be just as traumatic whether or not there is any warning. But at least you have time to say goodbye and resolve any issues still on the table between you and the dying person.

Other times, the loss is sudden and unexpected. You might tell yourself it is too soon. He or she shouldn't have died so young. What you really mean is that you aren't ready to let go of him or her. You feel cheated. Yet no one is guaranteed any particular amount of life nor are you guaranteed any length of time with those you love. Often this becomes a struggle or argument with God which we will consider a little later along with a few more thoughts on grief. Let's take a look at relationships next.

Who Is to Blame?

No one ever starts a relationship expecting conflict. Why would you bother? Friendship, dating and marriage all begin with both people feeling attracted to each other because they have something in common. Both parties see something in each other they would like to have as part of their lives. Sometimes it stays that way and the relationship deepens to their mutual benefit. But it doesn't always turn out that way.

Remember earlier when I described all living things as changing and growing over time? The same is true of any two people in a relationship. Everything is fine as long as you change and grow in complimentary ways. Sometimes you start to grow in different directions. Your values and beliefs might change to the point that out and out conflict results.

You are faced with another choice. You may feel hurt and rejected but not say anything. Or you could try to change yourself to make the relationship work. Yet you still might never quite come to an agreement about what you want from each other or are willing to give. No matter how both of you act or react, something must change in order to restore your inner balance. That in itself is stressful no matter how you approach your differences.

Death of a Relationship

Ideally your relationships will continue to deepen as you provide each other with comfort and companionship for the rest of your lives. You, as well as all other living things, including people, continue to grow and change throughout life. If a relationship is to survive, you both need to adjust and adapt to the changes in each of you in order to keep the relationship meaningful to both of you.

Sadly, not all relationships stand the test of time. Not everyone takes the trouble to keep their relationships up to date. People in any partnership, from an acquaintanceship to marriage, can, and sometimes do, outgrow the relationship to the point where it is no longer worth the effort to maintain it.

If no resolution can be reached, the relationship might well end, often with hard feelings on the part of one or both parties. Mutual blame can also hang in the air as well as feeling hurt, betrayed, angry or perhaps unappreciated.

Blaming yourself for the breakup distracts you from the business of getting on with your life and leaves a hole in your life where a relationship once existed. Blaming the other person leaves you angry and sometimes preoccupied with thoughts of revenge for his or her betrayal of you. But you can also think of what you learned from the relationship and enjoyed about it rather than being upset by its failure. We will look more at judgments and troubling emotions a little later in this book.

Some relationships end with the death of one of the parties. People vary in how much they are affected by the death of those who are important to them. Usually the closer your relationship, the more it affects you. It is obviously easier to let go of an acquaintance than a spouse. After all, close relationships involve sharing more of you and expecting more from the other person than do casual ones. This is especially true if you shared expenses, assets such as homes or responsibility for children.

Another stressor is the reminder that no one will live forever. Depending on how you feel about your own eventual death, losing a friend or spouse might indeed be unsettling. If you have come to terms with your own mortality, it might be easier to accept the loss of those you care about.

Abrupt changes in your way of life are always stressful, especially when you must proceed without the support of someone you trusted to help you along your life path. Other stressors might not be quite as dramatic as the ones we just discussed. Yet they can also be quite disturbing to your emotional balance. Let's look at a few of them.

Dealing with Demands

People often set deadlines for themselves which create stress in their lives. Fortunately, if it's your timetable, you can always change it. It's a little harder if someone else sets a deadline for you. You might like to live according to a schedule you find comfortable. Or you might prefer to have no schedule at all and do what you want to when you are ready. What happens when someone else sets a schedule for you, leaving you feeling rushed or overwhelmed?

Perhaps someone expects something impossible from you. If you want to please the other person, you might try your best but fail to deliver the goods. You could also say you can't do it and risk disappointing the other person, possibly lowering their estimation of you.

Maybe you will refuse to do it because it's against your principles. Then it's time to renegotiate what you expect from each other. Negotiating new expectations would be the most sensible approach, but relationships are not always sensible no matter how old you are.

When I was eleven, I read the male part in a play while a girl classmate read the female part. I did not know her very well before that, but we soon became fast friends and spent a fair amount of time together after school. One day she called to invite me to an opera which she and her parents were attending. I had already been dragged to an opera by my parents and hated every moment of it. I liked spending time with Rose but did not relish the idea of wasting time at another opera. I told her I could not make it.

I felt good about escaping the ordeal of another opera but felt bad about disappointing her. Later I learned to like and appreciate opera and wondered whether that would have happened sooner if I had accepted her invitation. I drifted away from her after that. I also wondered what would have become of our childhood relationship if I had said yes.

Your Bankbook

Some people grow up in families where money is a constant source of stress. Most of us have faced a financial crisis at one time or another. Growing up, I never worried about having enough to eat or whether our family would lose our house. In college I remember looking under the couch cushions for loose change to buy something to eat. I often made do with ramen noodles and once resorted to "one whole chicken in a can." The can appeared more edible than the chicken.

Money problems can be a minor inconvenience when you don't have ready cash for an outing. Major stress results from lack of enough money for food or the monthly rent. Short term financial crises invite worry. Extended periods without funds or prospects of any arriving soon can drain you emotionally.

Sometimes poor planning and failure to budget for expenses create financial stress. Using credit cards to buy things and then hoping to find enough money for the next bill sets you up for stress. Unexpected financial downturns can put you into crisis mode immediately despite your budget plans.

Finances are high on the list of stressors for many people. No individual has control of the economy. Everyone is affected by its ups and downs from the rich to the poor. For some people, it is a question of survival for themselves and their families. For others, it means rethinking what is important in life and perhaps setting new priorities or even changing their standard of living.

Job Loss

Job loss is one of the leading stressors in life. The main question is how you and your family will survive. How will you feed and care for yourself and your family if you have one? Will you be able to find a comparable job? What skills do you have to offer as a future employee?

Sometimes money is the least of your problems. Perhaps you have savings, a spouse who can take up the slack for a while or family and friends who can help out until you get back on your feet. What about the emotional impact?

Maybe you didn't get laid off but were fired. Perhaps you were told that you were not keeping up with the expectations or your employer or were not working hard enough. How easy is it to accept such criticism even if it is just implied rather than stated openly? Maybe you can hide what happened from others, but how do you feel about being pushed aside, whether or not your employer's assessment of you is fair?

Even if you are laid off due to no fault of your own, how do you feel about yourself now? You are no longer needed and there is no place in your former company for what you have to offer. It may now be difficult for you to approach job interviews confidently. What if you are rejected again?

Perhaps you have planned and saved for years to open your own business and then it fails. The great majority of new ventures fail in their first year, but that is not much consolation when it is you who falls flat on your face. What about all your plans and dreams for the future?

Old Age

Very few people look forward to old age. Yet many anticipate a point in their lives when they no longer have work commitments and can do as they please with their time. This assumes that they have a purpose to pursue as they age. You might become comfortable with a more relaxed lifestyle or you could become restless and disoriented without any external direction or context.

Growing older and retiring brings with them their own set of problems and stressors. Although illness can beset you at any age, I have met people who worked for years anticipating the adventure of freedom as they aged, only to find themselves dealing with a whole set of new problems they never planned for in terms of their personal health. Your body might not be up to the adventures you had so carefully planned.

Stigma

The early Greeks cut or burned a mark into a person's body to indicate that he or she was blemished in some way and less of a person. Slaves were marked on the Southern plantations when slavery was a booming trade and an economic benefit to many slave owners. *The Scarlet Letter* tells the tale of an adulteress shunned by her community and forced to wear a red "A" sewn onto her dress for all to see every time she went out in public.

Over the years, stigma has taken a wider meaning than just a mark on a person. Now it means the disgrace itself rather than just an outward mark. Some personal stigmas carry their own outward marks and are obvious to others such as blindness or deformity. More observant people look beyond the stigma carried by someone to discover the person behind the stigma. Yet many others still look down on those who are different from how they see themselves and view them as inferior.

Character blemishes or shortcomings can also provoke a stigmatizing reaction from others to varying degrees. Consider crime. A person who commits a misdemeanor carries a minor stigma while a felon carries a larger stigma. Various felonies carry greater or lesser degrees of stigma even among prison populations.

"Normal" people pride themselves as being above the level of those stigmatized in various ways. Religious stigmatizing reached an absolute frenzy during the Inquisition in Europe and at the time of the Salem Witch Trials in New England where heretics and witches were burned at the stake.

People can also be stigmatized through no fault of their own. Sexually abused children, the poor and those with different skin color or accents have been stigmatized by those who consider themselves normal or even superior. In contrast, some people born with birth defects in traditional primitive societies were seen as having special powers and significance. They were regarded most tenderly. Not so today in modern western civilization.

Other Random Stressors

I have described a variety of circumstances and happenings which bring uninvited stress into your life. This is not by any means the sum total of stressors which might sneak up on you during your life. I am sure you can think of many others. But you get the idea. Believe it or not, sometimes you choose to invite stress into your life. How? We'll get to that in the next chapter. Keep reading.

Life Lab Lessons

- **How did your family affect your values?** What did you believe as a child and who encouraged you to form these opinions?

- **How did your neighborhood shape you?** What do you think and feel about people in general? What happened in your neighborhood to lead you to your opinions?

- **What was important to your parents?** Do you still see the world the way they did? Or did something happen to make you see things in a different way? What happened?

28

- **What did you find stressful in your family?** How did you and your family members deal with stress? Did you even think of it as stress?

- **Have you lost important family members?** How did you react to it? Have you gotten over it? How?

- **What troubles did you face in relationships in the past?** Are you wrestling with any right now? How do these troubles affect you? Did you find a way to resolve the problems in the past? What helped?

Joseph G. Langen

Chapter 4- Stress by Choice

There's going to be stress in your life,
But it's your choice whether to let it affect you or not.

~Valerie Bertinelli~

What stressors do you choose? College, marriage, having and raising children, moving, changing jobs are a few of the possibilities. All of these life changes can be exciting. People often focus so much on the excitement that they overlook the stress involved. Change is a key to stress. So let's look at a few changes you might choose in your life.

Sports and Other Competition

One obvious stress you might choose is in the arena of competitive sports. As an individual or member of a team you face the possibility of winning or losing. Some people take this more seriously than others. You may just enjoy the game and don't care who wins or loses. At the other extreme you might look at competition as a way to prove your importance or self worth. If you win, you feel important. If you lose, you feel worthless. As a fan, you might feel like a success or failure depending on whether your team wins or loses.

When I was ten, a friend taught me how to play chess. I enjoyed learning the moves and what each piece could do. As I got a little better at the game, it started to feel like real life to me. If I was trapped into losing important pieces, I felt like my kingdom was at stake and it was my fault that it faced doom. Toward the end of games I eventually lost, I began to sweat and feel defeated even though it was just a game. I had invested part of my self worth in the outcome and risked it with each match.

College

College can be a major source of stress. This is another stress by choice, although it might not feel like a choice. Parents, teachers and peers might have expected you to follow high school with a stint in college. Flipping hamburgers or babysitting as a teen helps you to realize that you don't want to spend the rest of your life at a minimum wage job. It's time to look for something better and college seems the obvious way to accomplish your goal. Families, friends, or neighbors encourage college as a way for graduating seniors to improve their situation in life. Sometimes college seems like the only way up. Yet it's still a choice.

Like marriage, college at first seems like an adventure and it is. No more rules, no need to ask permission to do what you want to do, a chance to meet others, a whole world of possibilities, new friends, thinking for yourself. That's the great adventure part. Along with it comes new responsibility. No one asks if you did your homework. Teachers and parents no longer set standards for you to follow. You are on your own. Success or failure is in your hands.

Your newfound freedom feels great unless you screw it up and get carried away with the social side of college while letting your academics slide. What if you end up on academic probation, or worse, get kicked out of school. How do you explain that to your parents and friends? Now what do you do with your life?

Your Home

Where will you live? Moving out of your parents' home, you might choose apartment life as the most affordable option. You need to decide where you can afford to live, what kind of neighborhood you prefer and how you will get to work among other things. You will then consider what kind of lifestyle you have had in the past and whether you can continue it in your new home. If not, how easy will it be for you to find a way to live more affordably but still in a satisfying way?

You might buy a house. If you decide on a house, you will need to produce a down payment as well as commit yourself to years of mortgage payments. Also, what about the cost of upkeep and repairs that occur without any warning?

Work

Whether you go to college or not, sooner or later you will face the prospect of finding a job and supporting yourself. Perhaps you had a part time job in high school that led to a full time opportunity.

What about a career? Do you know what you want to do in life, and if you do, can you find a job in your chosen field of interest? Maybe you had a part time job in high school which you knew would be temporary. Now you are ready for a career.

I remember graduating with my Ph.D. in psychology at a time when jobs for psychologists were not very plentiful. Most of the ones I considered required professional experience which I did not have yet. But I needed a job to get that experience. Fortunately I had a classmate who was in high demand. Along with several other classmates, I took one of the jobs she left in her wake.

Finding a job can be very stressful, especially when you need the money to support a family. Once you're hired, you become part of a whole new world of expectations, regulations and traditions that make up the work culture where you work. You usually start at the bottom of the ladder and have to work your way up to the job you really want.

I graduated from the University of Illinois during the early 1970's, a time of great cultural change and of finding new ways to do things in the wake of the 1960's. Although I was glad to have any job, I found myself in an environment ruled by a person who had graduated from the college where I was hired and who had never worked anywhere except that very same college. Needless to say, her scope of knowledge about variety in the workplace remained quite limited.

New ideas I brought with me found a deaf ear. I wondered if I had survived my college and university days only to be put back in a rigid box of conformity. That was exactly the case and I had to endure my fate while I gained experience and sought help from friends to find a less rigid environment.

At work, you need to form some kind of meaningful working relationship with your supervisor if you want to survive. I know of one newly-hired person who had three supervisors at the same job. When she did something to the satisfaction of one supervisor, the other two were not pleased. She wound up moving on rather quickly.

Your coworkers might turn out to be your best supporters and help you become established in your position. Or you might have some competitive coworkers who see you as the competition and do their best to undermine your efforts to succeed in order to make themselves look good.

Moving On

Changing jobs carries its own stress. Should you discuss your plans with your supervisor? With your coworkers? What kind of reference will your supervisor give you? Will your new job be any less stressful than your current one or just more of the same? Will you be any happier after you move?

Finding a new job carries more stress if you were laid off or fired from your last job. We are talking about stressors you choose. Maybe you chose the wrong job in the first place. Often the stress is not so much over losing your job as over what to do next.

Maintaining your self confidence challenges you when you are no longer needed or wanted at work. Starting over is never easy. It might eventually work out for the best but it may not seem so at the time. And then there are the financial implications for you and your family while you are between jobs.

Relationships

You, like all humans, are a social being and life is easier to navigate when you have someone with whom to share it. You don't get to choose your family as we have seen, but you do choose your friends. Some potential friends might appear in your life by chance in the form of neighbors, coworkers, fellow volunteers or church members. Still, it is your choice to make friends or not. Some of these prospects may want to be friends with you. Then it is up to you to decide how much to let them into your life and how much of their lives you want to share.

People end up in proximity to you for many reasons. Some might remain acquaintances whom you encounter occasionally. If you like being around them, you may choose to get to know them better and eventually pursue a friendship. Some of these might develop into close friendships. How far you go in a relationship is up to you unless you give control of this to the other person.

Just like marriage partners, friends tend to change over time. Sometimes they change for the better and sometimes for the worse. Sometimes they are just different. You will come to appreciate some of your friends and rely on them to a great extent.

Some people you thought were friends could end up being toxic to you. They poison your environment including your own attitude toward life. Needless to say, stress accompanies this setback in your relationship, especially if you have come to depend on these people. Then it is up to you to set some boundaries and possibly end your relationship with them for the sake of your emotional well being or even your sanity.

You can form friendships at all stages in life from childhood through old age. Your friendships are usually based on common interests and ways of thinking. Not that you sit down and make a list of what you have in common. It usually happens gradually without much reflection on your part. Some relationships remain at the acquaintance level, such as with people you wave to when you see them, but they have no other involvement in your life.

Some of your relationships revolve around shared activities such as sports, church or clubs. Others progress to varying degrees of intimacy in which you share personal information about yourself, your life goals and mutually support each other with personal problems. Still others develop into relationships involving long-lasting, sometimes lifelong, commitment such as marriage or modern day alternative relationships.

So what's so stressful about relationships? Every time you get closer to someone, you share more personal information and trust your friend with part of your secret self. If you have ever had this backfire, you know what it feels like. In case you missed this adventure, it's no fun. Friendships are more likely to bring you stress when they come to an end. This is especially true if you feel a friend has betrayed your trust or feels betrayed by you regardless of what actually happened.

Dating

Dating is one of the activities we don't usually think of as stressful. Of course dating is exciting, it brings you to life and it leads you on a new adventure. But it's not all fun. Do you recall being attracted to someone in high school? You wondered whether he or she liked you too or even noticed you. If you spoke in his or her presence, how would you be received? You called your spy network into action to find clues about whether it was safe to approach the new object of your affection and whether that person might be open to your attention.

Even after your teen years, you might be skittish about dipping your toes into the water of the dating pool. You might be more than skittish if your previous relationship ended badly and you wonder if there is something wrong with you. Acceptance is a big deal especially if you long to trade your loneliness for companionship.

Tying the Knot

Traditionally, we think of a honeymoon as coming after the wedding. The truth is that the honeymoon period starts early in a relationship, often before marriage surfaces as a topic of conversation. The honeymoon can last months and even years after the wedding. You may know it as the gaga or infatuation stage.

People who date usually see each other only when they are at their best. They don't go on dates when they aren't up to it. Instead they stay home and wait until they feel better. Many people have a dark side which reveals itself only after the knot is tied and the marriage license is filed away.

Foremost in your mind is the excitement of a new relationship and having someone with whom to share your dreams, fears and interests. You look forward to mutual sexual delight, and relief of loneliness. Based on these improvements to your life, you might rush headlong into marriage without considering the rest of the package. I call this planning the wedding rather than the marriage.

What else is there to consider? Everyone has baggage from his or her previous life. Somewhere along the line, you might have been treated in ways that unsettled you. If you don't share these experiences and accompanying feelings with your spouse, you might well find yourself in a similar situation in your new relationship.

You might also unknowingly provoke old memories and feelings in your partner if he or she has not shared troublesome experiences with you. How can you avoid provoking each other if you don't know your mutual trigger points?

Reliving Old Patterns

Need an example? Okay, here's one. Suppose one or both of your parents were alcoholic and you felt powerless to do anything about it. You marry, hoping for a better relationship with your spouse than you had with your parents or than they had with each other. You might be determined to make it better to compensate for your miserable family life. Yet a few years after marriage, you discover that your spouse is an alcoholic. You are back where you started.

How could this happen? That's the last thing you ever wanted. Yet it is a very common experience. Unless you have had some help understanding alcoholism and addressing your feelings about it, you might have left your parents house with a sense of guilt about not having fixed their problem.

Since you are accustomed to an alcoholic environment, you might be attracted to a person who has similar tendencies as your parents or you might just be attracted to people who need to be fixed so you can finally feel better about yourself. You hope to fix him or her in a way you could not do for your parents.

Sometimes this works. More often than not the person you want to fix has no interest in being fixed. That reminds me of the story about a Boy Scout who came home with his uniform rumpled and torn. His mother asked him what happened. He told her he tried to help an elderly person cross the street. She asked how he ended up looking like he did. Sheepishly, the boy admitted that the person did not want to cross the street.

Your own agenda does not always match that of the person you wish to help. It is best to know what someone else wants so you don't sign up for a hopeless task.

Relationships with Eyes Wide Open

You need to understand yourself before jumping into a relationship like marriage. You also need time to learn about your potential spouse. What do you both want and need from the marriage? What can you give to each other? How well do these match? Do you complement each other?

Even if you take these precautions, you might forget that life is an ongoing process and that all sorts of changes await you. What you need from a spouse and have to offer to one is likely to change over the course of your

37

marriage. Your spouse will also evolve. A wise person I once knew told me that every marriage is either growing or dying.

Starting a marriage with your eyes wide open does not guarantee success. You must also stay in touch with your own and your partner's changing needs, wants and abilities and balance your lives from day to day to stay in harmony with each other. That's not always easy but it is well worth the effort.

As time goes by, a relationship can become routine. You might take it for granted and expect that it will always be the same. Yet a marriage is a living thing, just as each spouse is. It constantly changes whether you want it to or not. If you don't stay in touch with each other, you might end up thinking you are still living in a marriage which no longer exists.

Have you heard this story about a couple? A wife served liver and onions one Thursday night early in their relationship and her husband complemented her cooking. For years she served liver and onions every Thursday night. Finally the exasperated husband exploded, "Are you trying to torture me? Why do you insist on serving liver and onions every week? I'm sick of it! The astonished wife replied, "I never really liked them either but made them because you said you liked them." The equally astonished husband retorted, "I didn't like them. I just said that to make you feel good." Being open about their feelings from the start could have saved them both years of aggravation. Although seemingly trivial, the story demonstrates how small annoyances, left to fester, can lead to major rifts.

Family Additions

Couples often choose to have children. Some children are planned. Sometimes couples end up pregnant by mistake, being careless about birth control. The promise of a baby is often exciting as long as the prospective parents are emotionally and financially prepared for it.

Even when both spouses are mature enough to share their lives with children and are financially able to do so, they tend to be carried away by excitement over the new arrival and don't consider how it will change their lives.

Pregnancy and childbirth present challenges as well as excitement. Morning sickness, the mother's change in body image as well as possible medical complications often call for changes in how parents view their life together. As we have seen, change is one of the main ingredients in stress.

A carefree life gives way to responsibility for a baby. As much as parents love their baby, at times they will miss their old freedom.

Then there are the constantly changing fads in caring for babies and children:

- Should boys be circumcised?

- Should mothers breastfeed or bottle feed their babies?

- Should parents feed babies when they are hungry or on a schedule?

- Should they pick up crying babies or allow them to cry themselves to sleep?

No matter what you decide to do, some people will insist that you are wrong and that you should do the opposite of what you decide. You will hear plenty of well meaning but conflicting advice creating stress about whether you are doing the right thing.

Unless addressed, the change from being a couple to a family can add to the stress which parents experience from other parts of their lives. They then convey their stress to their children. Plato said that the unexamined life is not worth living. Knowing yourself and your spouse and maintaining communication determine whether major changes such as becoming parents will make your relationship stronger or weaker.

Divorce

As we have seen, many stressful situations arise for spouses during the course of marriage. Sometimes spouses are aware that they are making life more difficult for each other. Sometimes stressful situations cannot be resolved to their mutual satisfaction no matter how hard they try. We have already looked at some of these above and in the previous chapter. Now we come to the most stressful part of marriage, ending it. Here's why.

When relationships end, both parties might be broken-hearted for a while and wonder whether they will ever find someone else to love. Or perhaps the marriage ends because one of the spouses has already taken up with someone else and should not be surprised if this meets with anger on the part of the other spouse.

Sometimes they wonder whether pursuing another relationship is worth the effort. What if they fail again? Divorce presents even more challenges. Spouses each lose the person they thought they were closest to and who would always be there for them. Legal complications also result regarding their assets and rights regarding their children.

Divorcing spouses might own property together which needs to be divided. Even if they find an equitable and mutually agreeable way to settle this issue, they usually do not arrive at it without clawing and gnashing at each other, at least for a while. The courts also have something to say about the matter.

Although it might be nice to approach the situation rationally, at some point in the process spouses often become angry and nasty. They hire lawyers to fight on their behalf and neither spouse emerges feeling very good about the process even if the results are fair to both sides.

When there are children involved, it becomes even more complicated. Sometimes both parents fight forcefully to retain control of their children, losing sight of what is best for them and being more concerned about having their own way. This creates additional stress for parents and even more for their children.

For most spouses, the stress of divorce and all it implies compound their feelings of anger, disappointment, rejection, betrayal and just about any other negative emotion imaginable. At the marriage ceremony, each spouse professed their love for each other and vowed to accept each other no matter what. Divorce is often a tragedy for both spouses and a disappointment to their relatives and friends who are tempted to take sides in support of one or other of the spouses. A tangle of emotions often follows both spouses long after the divorce. Children can also feel devastated for years about the collapse of their family.

Retirement

After many years of marriage, with your children hopefully on their own or after years alone or in a relationship you reach the point where your work life comes to a close. Some people will work as long as they walk the earth. Most retire at some point even if to take a different kind of job.

Some people place all their eggs in the work basket. Their whole identity and purpose in life revolve around their career and making money. In that case, retiring might leave them without any sense of direction. Like fish out of water, they don't know what to do with themselves.

Retirement often means letting go of regular work relationships, some more important than others. Your work environment provides a context for at least part of your life. Once this is gone, you find yourself challenged to find a new meaning for your life.

Sometimes mandatory retirement is forced because of your age or your job might simply be phased out. Your work skills might no longer fit your company's needs. Hopefully, you will have thought about this long before it happens and have considered options for the next phase of your life.

Learning How to Say No

This challenge does not occur at any particular point on the timeline of your life. It can become an issue at any point and remain for years. But it usually starts in childhood as a way to get people to like you or leave you alone. When someone asks or demands something from you, how much choice do you feel you have in the matter?

You might feel that you are required to produce whatever anyone wants from you. Perhaps you were raised in this manner or maybe you didn't like the consequences you suffered in the past by saying no. Yet no matter how you feel about it, you always have the choice of politely declining, or insisting if it comes to that.

People you know can feel disappointed or even angry over your refusal. They may see you as selfish or ungrateful for what they have done for you in the past or just plain stubborn. There will be others who don't understand your reasons for saying no unless you tell them outright. You might have reasons you do not wish to share, which might inflame the situation or threaten your relationship if you did state them.

Here's an example. Suppose someone gets wind of your planning a trip to visit a dear friend whom you seldom see. You'd like to spend time talking with this friend about private matters between you and her or him. Then an acquaintance, with whom you are not comfortable sharing your secrets, asks to go with you.

Explaining all this to your acquaintance is likely to be uncomfortable and create friction rather than resolving the problem. "No" is a complete sentence and does not always require an explanation. You can make plans to spend time with your acquaintance later if you choose. Sometimes your best response is a simple "No." Don't make the mistake of going overboard meeting others' needs and leaving yourself in the lurch.

You are not a machine and do not have endless resources. Sometimes you are exhausted or just plain tired. Other times, you have your own stress to deal with. Or you just need to take a break. Codependence is a term from the chemical dependency field which has taken on wider meaning in our culture. It means going beyond your usual limits to take care of others and sometimes helping them to avoid taking responsibility for themselves for themselves. In the process, you do harm to yourself by taking on a thankless burden. Don't make that mistake!

You have physical, mental and emotional limits. Your body can do just so much before you become worn out. Figuring out how to be helpful to someone in a given situation can be emotionally draining. You don't want to become overwhelmed by someone else's needs especially if you don't know how you can help. Sometimes just listening is enough for the moment and it might give you some ideas about how you can be helpful.

Why would you feel the need to go to extremes to help others? Perhaps you came from a family in which your needs were not met on a physical or emotional level. You might come to see it as your mission in life to meet others' needs at all costs so others don't repeat your experience.

What if you came from a family in which you had a loved one who continued to struggle with an issue such as alcoholism despite your best efforts to save him or her? Having failed to save your loved one, you might be tempted to go in search of others whom you hope to save. Remember the lesson of the overly helpful Boy Scout above.

This might account for some people marrying a series of alcoholic spouses despite swearing they would never marry someone like their parents. People who think about it usually feel they have learned their lesson when their first marriage ended due to their partner's alcoholism. But continuing the same pattern in their next marriage happens all too often.

Maybe you took on the role of caretaker in your family while you were growing up, seeing it as your job to take responsibility for the rest of the family. Melody Beattie in her book, *The Language of Letting Go*, shares daily exercises to help you feel okay about being yourself. In another book, *Codependent No More*, she states that you don't need to depend on others for approval. Your self worth doesn't depend on how helpful you are to others. You don't need to overreact to everything in your life and you don't need to fix everything, especially if you didn't break it.

This is not to suggest that you should forget about everyone else and just take care of yourself. It is healthy to find a balance in your life, taking care of yourself first. If you don't, what will you have to offer others? Then look at how you can help others within the boundaries of your ability and while staying sane in the process. In looking to help others with their needs, you should consider whether you are capable of helping them, whether they really want or need your help, and whether they will appreciate your efforts.

Choosing Chemicals

I would venture to say that most people look to chemicals, legal or illegal, as ways to make themselves feel better or perhaps not feel anything at all. Regardless of your intentions, mind-altering chemicals you put into your body tend to upset your inner balance and, at the extreme, can kill you.

Two of the most dangerous drugs available today are legal: nicotine and alcohol. People often use them to diminish their stress in various situations. While they seem like an easy way to avoid or minimize stress, they invariably produce their own complications and more additional stress accompanying damage they do to your body.

Smoking

Nicotine, tar and the other chemicals in tobacco products do severe damage to your body, particularly to your heart and respiratory system. The Australian Better Health Initiative report indicates that tobacco contains over sixty cancer causing chemicals. Tar stains fingernails, teeth and lung tissue along its smoky path and delivers carcinogens or cancer-causing agents to your system. Carbon monoxide replaces oxygen being transported around your body. Tobacco smoke also irritates your trachea and larynx, reduces lung function and breathing while increasing the risk of lung infection.

In the circulatory system, these chemicals raise your blood pressure and heart rate, make blood clots more likely to occur, damage artery walls, reduce blood flow to your fingers and toes, and increase the risk of stroke and heart attack. They also affect your immune system by making you prone to pneumonia and influenza and lower the level of protective antioxidants like vitamin C.

Sexually speaking, chemicals increase the percentage of deformed sperm and contribute to impotence. In other areas of the body, smoking irritates the stomach and intestines, increases the risk of ulcers, inhibits your senses of smell and taste, wrinkles your skin, and increases the risk of blindness as well as gum disease.

43

Smoking while pregnant has been found to increase the risk of miscarriage, stillbirth and premature birth. It also contributes to low birth weight associated with an increased risk for the baby of eventual heart disease, stroke, high blood pressure, being overweight and developing diabetes. Second hand smoke can also endanger your baby.

Long term smoking increases the risk of a wide variety of cancers, lung disease, coronary artery disease and other heart problems, osteoporosis and hip fractures as well as circulatory difficulties in hands and feet. Can you find any stress here?

Alcohol- A Mixed Blessing

So what about alcohol? For quite a while the medical profession and the substance abuse treatment community debated whether or not alcoholism was a disease. Heavy alcohol abuse can lead to a variety of conditions and diseases, among them addiction to alcohol. Most people start drinking socially. Some carry their drinking to extremes in order to blot out difficult thoughts and emotions. Excessive drinking is a choice you make, sometimes not for very good reasons but still a choice. Many alcohol researchers and counselors today believe there is a genetic tendency to alcoholic addition which makes it easier for you or your children to become alcoholic.

Drinking alcohol initially relaxes you and then gives you a sense of euphoria and excitement. If you stop there, you don't usually suffer too many consequences. The problem is that the more you drink, the less control you have over the next drink. Your ability to choose becomes cloudy. Next the stakes get higher. Increasingly higher blood alcohol levels lead to inability to think clearly, paralysis of brain function, coma and ultimately death if you keep going long enough. You also have less control of your behavior and are more prone to doing things you would not do sober.

Recent studies suggest that limited use of alcohol can have some health benefits. But long term excessive use of alcohol can affect almost every part of the body. Among the effects are malnutrition, chronic pancreatitis, liver disease, cancer, nervous system disruption as well as affecting brain function.

Alcohol addiction traps you in a need to maintain a high level of blood alcohol. Even if you stop drinking or cut back on the amount you drink, you may be at risk of serious medical complications and possibly seizures.

For a comprehensive treatment of alcohol disorders and treatment, see Jean Kinney's book, *Loosening the Grip*.

Getting High

Although not often making the front page these days, death from heroin addiction is still rampant. Our culture is also laced with a variety of other illegal drugs, new ones being discovered or invented every day. It would take a whole book to chronicle the short and long term effects of all the drugs available in our communities and then it would be quickly outdated.

Quality control is not a high priority in this particular business. Very little of what reaches the street arrives in a pure state. Drugs are often cut with who knows what. Experimentation with drug combinations for a new variation on the experience of getting high leaves you open to unknown and usually not very happy results.

We have become a drug seeking culture. It is not uncommon these days to come home from the dentist, doctor's office or hospital with oxycodone rather than aspirin. Using such drugs, even for the most legitimate of reasons, is flirting with the slippery slope of addiction. Once you find yourself on this course, you have not just a taste but a mouthful of stress.

For much more on addictions, see Carl Hart and Charles Ksir's book, *Drugs, Society and Human Behavior*.

Food Addiction

It would be hard these days not to notice the epidemic of obesity and chronic conditions such as heart disease and diabetes overtaking our society. There is even a new medical term, "diabesity." Eating food in itself is not an addiction. After all, you need it to stay alive. At one time, it was thought that conditions like obesity and diabetes just happened to people randomly, perhaps due to bad luck or bad genes.

It is becoming increasingly clear that many of these conditions result from our culture's preoccupation with fast, easily prepared foods or ones handed out at a drive-thru window. Fat, salt and sugar have become entrenched as our first resort for comfort. Such foods and quasi-foods are known as comfort food. Refined carbohydrates such as white flour and sugar, high fructose corn syrup and refined grains all turn quickly to the simple sugar glucose which satisfies your taste buds if not the rest of your body.

Recent findings have found that these simple sugars have the same effect on the pleasure centers of your brain as heroin and cocaine and easily create a tolerance leading you to need more and more sugar to achieve the same effect. For more on this topic, see Kelly Brownell and Mark Gold's book, *Food and Addiction: A Comprehensive Handbook*.

Other Chemical Risks

So far, we have considered physical effects of the various drugs you might consume. You should not overlook the mental and emotional risks these chemicals bring with them. None of these drugs come to you free of complications for very long. Keeping supplied takes money away from your other needs, usually adding to financial stress.

This does not include the cost of treatment for medical problems caused by drug abuse. Then you have emotional isolation, the deterioration of your relationships with others, the toll of becoming involved in the legal system and possible effects on just about any other aspect of your life you can think of.

Choosing Toxic People

Now that doesn't make much sense, does it? Why would you choose to have toxic people around you? First of all, what are toxic people? I mentioned them briefly above. You know about toxic chemicals kept in bottles with skull and crossbones warning labels. Without such labels, how would you know they were toxic? Hopefully not by trying them!

People of interest here don't come with labels or signs around their necks saying, "I'm toxic. Keep your distance." Do you recall my mentioning spouses who escape from their first marriage to an alcoholic only to take up with another alcoholic and wonder why they do it? We talked about this earlier on when we discussed reliving old patterns.

Recall the definition of stress as your reaction to a demand for change. People tend to stick with the familiar in their lives to avoid the stress of a new situation. Finding someone similar to your former spouse feels familiar but often lands you back where you started with the same

46

problems and the same stress. This vicious circle can plague your attempt to find a new relationship unless you spend some time understanding what happened the first time around.

When a relationship with a friend, relative, dating partner or spouse deteriorates, you feel fortunate when it ends. If you don't stop to examine what went wrong and why you found that person toxic, you are likely to drift into another similarly toxic relationship.

Fortunately you get to choose the people with whom you associate. It might not be easy to end a relationship or limit it to the bare necessities. Yes, setting boundaries around yourself and your living space will involve some stress and perhaps will not be well received. But compare it with the stress of continuing a toxic relationship and living with a millstone around your neck. Take it off! For more about starting over after leaving relationships which do not work, see Bruce Fisher and Robert Alberti's book, *Rebuilding When Your Relationship Ends*.

Guilt

You don't exactly choose to feel guilty, at least not directly. Yet guilt is mostly based on choices you make and on your actions. Guilt is partly a judgment you make about yourself. You judge yourself as falling short of your personal values and standards or the standards of a group or organization with which you identify. For a small infraction, you might feel a brief twinge of guilt and hope to do better next time around. You might also experience extreme guilt for major transgressions and have difficulty ever forgiving yourself.

Guilt might also be a judgment imposed on you by your religious beliefs or government to which you are attached. You might be shunned or condemned by a religion, or fined or incarcerated by a government. In either case, you are judged guilty and suffer the consequences for your choices.

But guilt is not just a judgment by you or someone else. It is also a feeling which might lead you to decide that you let yourself or your group down. You might also feel like a lesser person because of what you did.

Guilt might also embrace you without any action on your part. This is called guilt by association. The police might judge you guilty of a crime if you are with others who are caught, whether or not you actually participated in it. You might also find yourself sharing a sense of guilt with family, friends, your ancestors, your community or government who act in ways which do not follow accepted community standards or your personal ones.

There are people whom others judge as guilty but who have no sense of remorse. They don't apologize, take any responsibility or feel the least bit bad about what they did. These are known as antisocial individuals who give no more than lip service to public standards. If caught, they deny what they did, make excuses or blame someone else. We will further consider the feelings associated with guilt in a later chapter.

Overbooking Yourself

You have most likely seen the confusion in airports when flights are overbooked. No matter how it is handled, nobody is particularly happy about the results. You might overbook yourself in your daily routine or become disorganized in other ways.

True, following a schedule can feel stressful and confining. Yet, without a plan, you are likely to find yourself wandering in circles from time to time. How will you get to where you are going if you don't know where you are headed and how you will get there? You will hear more about organization later when we get to managing stress.

Other Stressful Choices

I have mentioned a few of the more common ways in which you choose stress or leave yourself open to it. There are many others. Some are of little consequence and are of passing concern. Others might accompany major life choices bringing with them a great deal of stress. Anticipating the stress which accompanies your choices might help you decide whether the stress is worth enduring to accomplish your goals.

During the last Olympics, I listened to quite a few athletes being interviewed about their upcoming events. Almost universally, they admitted significant stress over how they would perform even after years of preparation and practice. For them the stress was worth it for the opportunity to earn an Olympic medal or at least to compete for one.

Obviously you don't choose every stressor which turns up in your life as you saw in the last chapter. Many of them are entirely out of your control and you could not have anticipated or avoided them. You had no choice in the matter.

You have also seen in this chapter some of the stressors you choose to accept into your life as the price to be paid to accomplish your goals. Regardless of whether they ambush you or you choose them, you do have a choice of how to think about the stressors you encounter, how to react to them and how to use them to your benefit in the future. Next we will turn to how stress affects you. But before we do, let's stop once more to take stock of your choice to take on stress.

Life Lab Lessons

- **Can you think of stressors you chose without realizing it?** Sometimes you don't think about the choices you make until you are already living with the consequences. What might those be for you?

- **What were the best choices you made in your life?** Think about how they made your life better or easier. What would your life be like now if you did not make these choices?

- **What were the worst choices you made in your life?** How did you happen to make these choices? What consequences did you face? Could you have prevented them? How? What steps have you taken to make sure you don't end up there again in the future?

- **Have your relationships been troubled by chemical or other addictions?** Is the problem your own use or that of someone close to you? Have you come to terms with the problem? How? If not, what can you do now?

- **Can you think of any stressful choices you have made which we have not discussed**? Are they still a problem? If so, what plans do you have for tackling them? If you don't have any plans, ask someone you trust for suggestions.

Joseph G. Langen

Chapter 5- Stress and Your Body

It is not stress that kills us; it is our reaction to it.

~Hans Selye~

So far we have talked about what stress is and where it comes from. The original scientific research on stress centered on what stress does to the body. Let's look at what happens inside your body when stressors descend on you or when you invite them into your life.

Back to the Roots

You might remember from the first chapter that Selye brought stress to the attention of the medical community. He saw it as, "a non-specific response of the body to any demand for change."

Let's look a little closer at his definition. Selye wrote about a non-specific response. The body does not have a word for stress. Nobody calls up your brain and says, "Hey, we have an emergency here." Instead, your nervous system carries an electrical signal through your nervous system to the brain saying that something out of the ordinary is happening.

If you receive a strong enough signal, you might well react to a stressor before it even reaches your awareness. For example, if you touch a hot stove accidentally, your sensory-motor circuits remove your hand from the stove before you even know what happened. Then you feel pain.

Messages make their way through your nervous system and blood stream warning your various organs to put on their helmets and take their battle stations. Like many military men, specific parts of your body are not informed of the exact nature of the danger. Yet your body flies into action in response to whatever is going on. Next, let's see how your body deals with a stressor.

Your Stress Antenna

Not everyone reacts the same way to stress. Of course people react differently to all other developments as well as stress. Some people go into a tailspin every time something goes wrong or when life does not follow the script they think it should. Others seem unflappable no matter what happens. Most people's reactions lie somewhere in between. Take some time to consider where you fall in the continuum.

Explanations for these differences lie on several levels. As they do in most other aspects of your life, your genes contribute to your stress response. But this is not the whole story. As your life progresses, you learn ways to react which your family considers normal. That does not mean that these reactions are necessarily normal, but that's just how things are done in your family.

Quite a few years might pass before you stop to wonder if you could handle things in a different way than your family was accustomed to. Did you know that children of deaf parents learn not to cry when they are uncomfortable? What's the point? Instead they learn more visible ways to react in order to get their parents attention.

Let's get back to what happens in your body in times of stress. Your body has no email, texting privileges or Facebook page. You learn of stressors through your senses, the same way you learn about everything else going on around you. Sometimes you talk yourself into a stress reaction without any input from the outside, but that's a topic for another chapter. You can see, hear taste or smell danger approaching. You can also bump into it literally when you feel an assault on your body. Sensory nerves carry electrical messages to the brain which in turn alerts the rest of your body to danger and sends the troops into action.

In case of sudden danger like a stove burning your hand, your system can't wait for a considered response from the general, your brain. The sergeant at arms in the spinal cord orders immediate action through your motor nerves in parts of the body needed for quick response. Meanwhile, the message continues along the chain of command, eventually arriving at the brain for further evaluation. Okay, so you have taken immediate action and the situation has been reported to your brain. Now what?

The Body at War with Stress

Fortunately, your body has an excellent emergency response system. Your nervous system handles the initial response, like a first responder administering first aid. If the stressor cannot be handled immediately, you also have an intricate network of electrical and chemical messengers reaching all parts of your body to prepare it for battle. You might wonder how the body reacts the way it does. Let me explain in a little more detail.

When you are under attack, your pupils dilate to let in more light so you can better see what the problem is. Many of your emergency responder systems, such as your muscles, need glucose, or sugar, for fuel to fight the intruder or beat a hasty retreat in the face of insurmountable odds.

Stopping for a snack while the body is under attack would not be very timely. Fortunately your liver has a store of fat reserves which can be converted into glucose through a process known as glucogenesis. The adrenal glands, alerted to the presence of stress, send the hormone cortisol to the liver to get the process started so more glucose will circulate in the blood stream to feed the hungry army of stress responders.

Your lungs switch into high gear, working overtime to increase the oxygen supply to your various systems. Blood pressure and heart rate also join the effort to keep the supplies of glucose and oxygen moving. Adrenalin is released into your blood stream, not surprisingly by the adrenal glands, and circulates around your body to alert the troops that something is wrong and to prepare for action, either fight or flight. Increased glucose in the blood stream makes your brain more alert and prepares muscles for defensive action if needed.

In addition to calling up the reserves, non-essential activities are suspended. As in any war, activities not strictly necessary for the battle are put on hold. Your digestion grinds to a halt, your immune system shuts down for a while and sexual arousal is put aside for some other time. Glucose enriched blood rushes to all parts of the body to nourish the troops preparing to deal with stress.

Your Body on Continuous Alert

In theory, this high alert is a temporary state lasting until the threat is under control. Your brain moves quickly to decide whether to beat a hasty retreat or to stand and fight. This state of heightened alert is meant to handle immediate stressors. When all goes as planned and the stress is avoided or resolved, the troops stand down and the body resumes its normal activities.

But what happens if the stress does not go away? Your body is left in a state of chronic stress. So now what? Using the war analogy, troops indefinitely on high alert become exhausted and depleted. The body has a similar reaction to chronic stress. It grows weary of standing on guard, not knowing when or if action will take place.

I just mentioned digestion stopping during periods of stress. Your digestive system relies on blood to deliver nutrients to the rest of your body. If most of your blood is drawn to your brain and muscles, it can't at the same time serve the digestive system to pick up more nutrients. This is fine in an emergency and the liver provides energy from its reserves, but it's a different story in the face of chronic stress.

As a result of chronic stress, you might not feel hungry enough to eat. The digestive process is thrown off and you might develop difficulties such as ulcers or bowel problems like diarrhea or constipation. These difficulties interfere with your daily functioning and keep you uncomfortable to say the least. At worst your body ends up in a state of turmoil.

I also mentioned the immune system shutting down. Germs are not the main priority when your very existence is at stake. You can manage for a while without your immune system functioning at full capacity.

Here is just one example of what can happen. Being chronically on alert keeps your blood sugar, glucose, at a high level. The pancreas produces more insulin to help cells absorb the glucose. In turn cells become resistant to insulin after a while. Over a period of time, you end up with a condition called diabetes. I am not suggesting that stress is the only cause of diabetes, but it's one of the main contributors to developing this condition.

Long term stress can also lead to a few other problems:

- Fuzzy thinking or trouble making decisions.

- Thyroid trouble.

- Decreased bone density and muscle tissue.

- Chronically elevated blood pressure.

- Reduced immunity to disease.

- Decreased ability to heal from wounds.

- Increased abdominal fat which acts as a storage depot for the excess blood sugar circulating in your blood stream.

- Abdominal or belly fat is associated with heart attacks, strokes, elevated triglycerides and low density lipoprotein, also known as LDL or too much "bad fat", in your blood stream.

Smoke Signals

You don't directly experience your body's struggle to cope with chronic stress. You can't always tell if your inner workings have gone awry. But your body does signal that all is not well. These signs might be more obvious to others than they are to you. Remember the Johari window in Chapter 2?

Here are some ways the body signals that it is under stress:

- Stooped posture suggests fatigue.

- Sweaty palms can also give away inner stress.

- Stress interfering with your sleep or nutrition can leave you exhausted.

- Staying on high alert from stress with your sleep and nutrition out of balance can also contribute to a feeling of chronic fatigue, lack of alertness, memory difficulty, tension or pain in your muscles and chest.

- Sure to get your attention, or maybe your partner's attention, is lack of interest in sex or difficulty with sexual performance even if you are aroused.

These signals are the body's way of telling you it is off kilter. They are warning you to be alert to them and suggesting that you pay attention to your inner workings to see what is wrong. If you can't figure out what is wrong by yourself, you can check the millions of online citations for all the information and opinions about stress available on the Internet.

You may also want to discuss these signs of stress with your friends or health provider. Handling your stress earlier rather than later can save you quite a bit of trouble and maybe your life. It also saves you significant wear and tear on your body.

In addition to the physical signs of stress, your emotions, behavior and mental state can also warn you of trouble brewing under your skin. We will look at them a little later. In the next chapter, we will consider what happens in your mind as a result of chronic stress. Again, remember that not everyone reacts the same way.

Life Lab Lessons

- **Where do you first feel stress?** Do you get headaches, stomachaches, or feel tense? People react differently from stress. One theory is that stress attacks the weakest part of your body. Consider it an early warning system. Once you know stress is brewing, you will be more likely to head it off at the pass rather than letting it torture you and paralyze you.

- **Do you frequently come down with minor ailments?** You can't see your immune system, but if stress is keeping it from working efficiently, you will be more vulnerable to frequent colds, infections, stomach upsets and flu. This is a sign that you might have more stress in your life than you think.

- **How much attention do you pay to the signals your body sends you?** Do you take these signals seriously or ignore them, hoping they will go away? They are there for a reason. It would be best to look into them.

- **What if stress remains after you deal with it?** This could mean one of two things. You might have more stress than you thought and need to keep working on it. The other possibility is that you could have more than one source of stress. Resolving one does not mean that you don't have other issues to work on.

- **What can I do to avoid stress rather than cleaning up the mess after it hits me?** An excellent question. You can't always avoid stress but there are some things you can do to minimize it and prevent it. We will spend a whole chapter looking at how a little later.

Chapter 6- Stress And Your Mind

Stress is nothing more than a socially acceptable form of mental illness.

~Richard Carlson~

Psychological stress is different from bodily stress. We just saw how stress affects your body. Psychological stress results not only from what happens to your body. It also arises from how you think about it, what you sense is happening to you or what you imagine is happening.

Your thoughts do not always come from the reality surrounding you but might be something you concocted in your mind almost like science fiction. People don't go out of their way to upset themselves, but sometimes they do it anyway. Imagination is a great thing but you can be carried away by it.

In the case of acute stress, your nervous system, which we discussed earlier, sometimes produces a reaction before you have a chance to think about what happened. But during periods of prolonged stress, you can talk yourself into a helpless state, leading to patterns of depression, anxiety, and aggression which you drag around with you as well as your burden of stress.

When someone tells you, "It's all in your head," it sounds like your reaction to stress is a figment of your imagination. You might hear that it's time for you to stop being silly and get real. Yet your thoughts can create consequences for your whole being whether or not you see things the way others do and regardless of whether your concerns are real or imagined.

People who commit suicide usually think about it before attempting it. They might make what is known as suicide gestures. These are acts which are self-harmful but not intended to be fatal. Suicide gestures are a desperate measure designed to get others to take your suffering seriously. If no one takes your distress seriously, you might be tempted to escalate to a full-blown suicide attempt with the intention of actually ending your life. Some people go too far with gestures and end up dead in the process. Suicidal thoughts are best taken seriously.

You have the ability to look ahead before acting, to think about what you are doing while you are doing it and to later evaluate what you did to see if it was a good way for you to act. You can use your mind this way when it is functioning normally. That doesn't mean that you will always use your thinking to your own benefit. But it's nice to know that you at least have the capacity to do so.

Sometimes you have no trouble identifying stress in your life and can see clearly that stress is a problem for you. Living with stress for a long time can dull your awareness of being stressed and after a while you might no longer recognize that you are living under stress at all. Here are some more signs that stress is a problem even if you think you are doing fine:

- Worrying all the time.
- Feeling overwhelmed with life choices, and being unable to control your life.
- Feeling that your emotions control you rather than help you.
- Forgetting important tasks including taking care of yourself.
- Fearing situations which you used to take in stride.
- Turning to self medication such as alcohol, drugs or overeating.

Now let's see what stress can do to your mind. For years, psychologists and psychiatrists have argued about whether there is such a thing as a mind. Maybe what you think of as thought is it just a matter of brain circuitry and electrical impulses as you respond to stimuli in your environment. What's your thought on the matter?

I am of the opinion that you do have a mind and that your awareness of your world is separate from the mechanics of how your brain works. I also agree that brain problems can confuse your thinking. The research seems clear that your mind and brain are interconnected even if separate.

We discussed earlier how your body reacts to generalized stress. Your adrenal glands do not know what the problem is, only that there is an emergency requiring a response. Your mind tries to make sense of this emergency. You want to understand what is happening so you can respond appropriately.

It makes a difference whether a cat knocks over a vase or whether the house is falling down around you. Both might startle you, but one is far more serious than the other. Thinking about it can help you decide how strongly to react and what actions to take.

We have seen that your body can react to immediate stressors even before your brain receives a danger signal or your mind understands what happened and what the implications are. With immediate stress, you can address the problem and get back to business as usual right away, or at least fairly soon. In the last chapter, we saw that chronic stress takes a heavy toll on many body systems. The mind can become equally stressed as well.

The Brain-Mind Connection

As you may recall, chronic stress draws on all your body's resources over a period of time, depleting your reserves and weakening your ability to respond over time. The brain is no exception to stress's victims.

Your brain has the job of staying informed about what goes on around you. It collects information from your senses which it uses to direct how your various body organs and even your cells react. Your mind interprets the meaning of your stress. It also decides on a longer term plan to cope with stress on an ongoing basis if the stressful situation is not resolved by an immediate response.

Let's consider an example. Say you took a test in a difficult course and received a grade of D. This is a required course which you must pass in order to graduate. Getting a D makes you wonder whether you will even pass this course with its implications for your future.

After your immediate panic, you realize that something has to change. Maybe you need to spend more time studying or perhaps you need a tutor to get through this course. No matter what you decide, you have quite a bit at stake. You weigh your options and hopefully make a wise decision.

We saw that after an extended period of high alert, your brain and the rest of your body become exhausted. You may have trouble sleeping or you might fall asleep at inopportune times. I am sure you have heard what happens to soldiers on guard duty when they become exhausted. Perhaps you have had that experience yourself.

Disruption of your digestion can deprive your brain of needed glucose. When your brain grows weary, your mind doesn't work very well either. Let's look more closely at what chronic stress can do your mind.

Your Mind in a Fog

The psychologist William James stated that to an infant the world appears as "blooming, buzzing confusion." Everything is new. You don't know what to make of anything or how to react to it. You gain experience with your world as you grow up. Your mind uses what you learn to see patterns in various situations. In turn you learn how to react appropriately after a few tries. At least that's the hope, although some people do a better job making sense of themselves and their world than others do. Here is what chronic stress does to your mind:

- When you weary of stress, any exertion can make your body feel like it is slogging through molasses. Your mind feels the same way when it is overtaxed.

- Your thinking becomes unpredictable and you can't count on your mind to stay focused.

- You can't rely on your mind to sort out problems or perhaps even make sense of them.

- Organizing the facts involved, seeing your options and deciding on the correct course of action all become more difficult.

- You can't seem to get your mind in gear as if you have become paralyzed mentally.

The amount of stress you feel varies from one moment to the next and from one situation to another. Perhaps something distracts you from the stress and your mind functions a little better at least for a while.

Then the stress returns to your awareness and you again fumble with your thoughts. You feel like you are on a mental roller coaster, sometimes thinking clearly and sometimes lost in a jumble of disconnected thoughts.

With your mind in a state of confusion, you have trouble knowing what is going on around you and you are not sure you can trust what you see and hear. You might slip back into experiencing your world with the baby's blooming buzzing confusion. If you are not sure what is going on, it will surely be hard for you to react appropriately to the situation in which you find yourself.

It's like walking into a room where everyone is arguing with everyone else. You don't know what, if anything, you should pay attention to. Words fly at you and you have trouble making sense of them. If someone takes you aside and asks you which opinion makes sense to you, how easy is it for you to form your own opinion while the shouting continues at full tilt?

Under stress, you can feel bewildered, even without anyone else present. You can see that uncertainty follows closely on the heels of confusion and you might like to take a break while you sort it all out. Yet in times of high or sustained stress, you don't always have the option to put the matter aside and ponder it for a while.

If you can't make sense of the situation, you are left with a sense of confusion and unpredictability as well. You have no idea what will happen next. How do you prepare for the unknown? You can't tie up what you experience in a neat bundle and put it aside while you go on with your life. Instead you remain off balance, not quite sure how to react.

Hair Trigger Reactions

You can also develop the habit of overreacting to just about everything. When your mind is on high alert, anything that happens can seem like an emergency. Forgetting to mail a letter makes you think you have lost your mind. How could you be so absent minded?

Overreacting might take the form of making mountains out of molehills. Under ordinary circumstances, you would know that this particular stressor is not such a big a deal. But since you are not thinking clearly, you react as if it is a big deal. It doesn't help matters any, but you struggle to keep everything in balance without becoming further confused.

Even when you don't overreact, you can still act on impulse. Perhaps you don't make a great choice but at least you feel better doing something rather than doing nothing at all. You might regret your decision later or you might not. Regardless of how it turns out, you have not had time to think it through in order to make a considered decision.

You don't always connect your mental difficulty with stress. You can become so accustomed to living in a stressful situation that you forget this is not your normal state. You might wonder what is wrong with you, fear you might have a brain tumor or be on a slippery slope toward senility.

Engaging Your Memory

One reason you might overreact or act on impulse is a problem with your memory. With your mind focused on a real or imagined emergency, all of your attention is on the perceived threat. You might forget that you faced a similar threat in the past. If you did remember, you might have a better idea what to do this time.

Sometimes, if your stress level is not too great, your memory might eventually sharpen and help you out of a jam or remind you that you can manage this situation. But as you feel increasing stress, your memory

61

becomes less available and less helpful. Your ability to weigh a situation, make judgments about it and decide on an appropriate action all suffer under severe stress.

A high degree of stress not only limits your ability to act appropriately but makes it harder to do any kind of thinking at all. Next time you are under stress, try solving some mathematical problems. Or maybe not! Just take my word for it.

In a state of chronic stress, you tend to ignore important matters to which you would ordinarily attend carefully. You withdraw from concentration on work or school. You might not pay much attention to people you care about. You also attend less to your own needs, becoming sloppy with your personal appearance and hygiene. Many animals can smell fear and distress in other animals. There seem to be times when we can smell it on ourselves as well.

Down in the Dumps

You probably guessed that it's time to talk about depression. You are right. The Mayo Clinic defines depression as a "mood disorder that causes a persistent feeling of sadness and loss of interest affecting how you feel, think and behave."

We will look more at the emotional side of depression in the next chapter. While sadness is a normal part of life for everyone at times, we are talking here about feelings which don't seem to be connected with your daily events. Depression also affects your thinking.

Depression can take over your life, dragging you down to the dregs of existence no matter how well your daily life treats you in other areas. You come to see your life as worthless and give up trying to change anything. Depression can alternate with periods of normal functioning or with manic episodes marked by fuzzy thinking and erratic behavior.

While your reaction to stress depends in part on your genes, the neuroendocrinologist Robert Sopolski notes that your experience of stress also depends on what happened in your early years. He sees attitudes about life held by other family members as also making a difference in how you react to everything including stress later in life.

What if you grew up in a family with pessimistic parents who gave up on life ever getting better and spent their days wallowing in misery? You can imagine how this might incline you to see managing your life as a hopeless task. You might end up thinking that, no matter what you do, your life must be endured rather than enjoyed.

Lack of outlets for frustration also adds to your inclination toward depression and its associated stress. There are plenty of ways to distract yourself from the stress of depression. If you can't think of any at the time, you are stuck with depression monopolizing your thoughts.

If you find depression descending on you on a regular basis, it might help to make a list of what makes you feel more cheerful at least for a while. When you find yourself in deep depression, it is not a particularly good time to do something as logical as making a list. It would be best to work on one when you are in a better mood and save it for when you really need it.

Isolation and feeling a lack of support from others can also keep you feeling stuck. Without feeling supported, you are left in your own private hell. You might have trouble seeing alternatives for yourself, but others might have some ideas you have not considered.

Don't convince yourself that you have to face everything on your own and that no one else cares. Friends you have made under better circumstances might well be helpful. They are more likely to come to your aid if you ask them for their help rather than just complaining about how bad things are. Nobody wants to help you feel sorry for yourself.

Lack of predictability also keeps you off balance. If you have no idea when certain stressors will attack you, you are more likely to withdraw into a shell to protect yourself from the barrage. Yet avoiding everything in your life leads to more isolation and loneliness as well as, you guessed it, more stress.

Feeling you have no sense of control also adds to your sense of helplessness. How positive would you feel about your circumstances if you found yourself in a boat on the high seas in the midst of a storm with no sail, rudder, oars or motor? It can feel like that when you are in the throes of depression. You have tools you can use. But you might have trouble remembering what they are under dire circumstances.

Depression becomes more likely if you are convinced that things can only get worse. It is tempting to give up when you don't think there is any chance of things getting better.

If you learn how friends deal with their depression, you will see that they often come out of it after a while and return to their former selves. They could find their own way out of the nightmare. Or others might come to their aid. They might consider counseling and medication. The same possibilities are available to you.

Be aware that depression is a mental illness. So how can you do anything about it on your own? Research has uncovered a genetic predisposition toward depression. In other words, it runs in families.

That does not mean that if your parents were depressed you will necessarily follow suit. What it does mean is that given a tendency toward depression, you are more likely to react with depression under conditions which produce chronic stress.

Perhaps you have noticed almost as many TV ads for antidepressants these days as for erectile dysfunction medications. You might be led to believe that depression is entirely a chemical condition in your body which medication can cure. Chemical imbalances certainly appear with depression. Yet your life circumstances make their own contribution and need to be considered as well as medical ways to manage depression.

As with many psychological conditions, genetic predisposition makes it more likely that depression will emerge under certain mental and emotional circumstances. Most researchers and clinicians agree that addressing life experiences as well as chemical imbalances is necessary when seeking treatment options.

Depression shows many faces. Here are a few:

- Lack of pleasure in anything
- Slowing of your thinking and reactions
- Changes in appetite
- Trouble sleeping enough or sleeping too much
- Changes in sexual interest or performance

All of these signs can produce stress in their own right, further increasing your sense of living under stress and of feeling depressed. Depression is not the only mental condition causing stress. Let's look at some others.

Facing Anxiety

Anxiety is a sense of foreboding often tied to fear of certain events happening. It can also be a generalized sense of impending misfortune or even doom seemingly unrelated to anything happening in your life right at this moment.

Over time anxiety can become a habit with no specific focus to your fear. In such a state you find yourself constantly looking over your shoulder or wondering, "What if..." This type of anxiety follows the confusion, uncertainty and unpredictability we discussed earlier as well as depression. Not only can anxiety result from stress, a steady diet of anxiety also increases your stress, creating a vicious circle.

In addition to generalized anxiety with no specific focus, a variety of specific kinds of anxiety lie in wait for you. Social anxiety occurs when you dread being with other people. It produces excess fear of being around others, whether the people involved are a regular part of your life or complete strangers, although it is more likely with strangers.

This fear might be based on your past experiences. You might have been bullied in school and learned to keep a low profile as a defense. You might have been betrayed by people you thought were your friends. Or maybe you have always been shy for one reason or another and concluded that you feel safer avoiding too much contact with others.

Obsessive compulsive disorder keeps you preoccupied with your thoughts or actions as you worry endlessly about everything from traumatic to unimportant events with trouble deciding which is which.

Those who suffer from it describe themselves as wanting to do everything right all the time. They constantly rehearse how they will react in almost every situation. When the event passes, they continue to ruminate about whether they handled it correctly and worry about why they might have made the wrong decision.

Obsessive thoughts can also lead to self doubt and concern about whether you are any good as a person. You might torture yourself with thoughts about mistakes you have made in the past and constantly fear that anything you do will be taken the wrong way by somebody if not everybody.

Post traumatic stress disorder follows from the experience of a traumatic event. The trauma might not even be yours. You might have observed something horrible happening to someone else. Paralyzing fear can follow reminders of the event and you can be easily startled or upset by its memory.

A graphic example of post traumatic stress disorder follows combat experience in which you are injured or see your companions injured or killed. For years after the war ends, your thoughts are taken back to your wartime experience by fireworks, airplane engines or anything else you associate with battle even though the events took place long in the past.

Then there is the variety of specific fears of everything from ablutophobia or fear of washing or bathing, to zoophobia or fear of animals. These fears are usually triggered by frightening experiences with the object of your fear, but can also stem from seeing others' scary encounters.

Stories you might hear can also increase fear of things you might never have experienced in person. For years I had a strong fear of root canals, thinking them to be among the most horrid experiences I could ever have. That is until recently when I had one and found it to be uncomfortable but not at all as traumatic as I had imagined.

Separation anxiety disorder is fear of being separated from a parent or caretaker. The diagnosis is generally reserved for children but also has an adult form. Such people have not been able to function independently throughout their lives.

When they no longer have someone to rely on, they are suddenly faced with the prospect of meeting the future on their own and being left to their own devices. Yet they feel that they do not have any skills to use in facing life's challenges.

Ads for anti-anxiety medication abound and scientists speculate that there might be a genetic predisposition toward anxiety as there is for depression. Medication can be helpful in serious cases but is not the sole approach.

It is clear that some people react quicker and more strongly to everything that happens to them, good or bad. You probably know people who become very excited about everything they experience. Maybe you are one of them.

This is a mixed blessing. Being more joyful is good but you also become sadder or angrier than others when life throws you a curve. This tendency could be genetic but, as with other conditions we have discussed, most likely early development and later life experience also make their contribution.

Our society has become one in which we expect quick and easy answers to everything. Dipping a toe into the waters of anxiety prompts you to look for immediate answers such as those promised by medication. However, there are more permanent and non-addictive approaches which we shall consider a little later.

Flying off the Handle

We haven't talked much about aggression so far. Quite a bit has appeared in the news lately about the link between aggression and testosterone. I remember learning in high school biology class that capons, surgically castrated poultry, tended to be fatter and more docile. Good for the poultry farmers, not so great for the capons.

What about for people. I'm not aware that castration has been tried as a cure for anger, although chemical castration has been tried for perpetrators of sexual abuse with varying degrees of success and quite a bit of controversy surrounding the practice.

Life circumstances can lead you to more aggressive acts than might be typical for you. Think about times when you are tired, sick or frustrated by a problem you can't solve. Or maybe your life just feels out of control.

If you are like most people, you tend to be edgy when this happens. Or you might find yourself being pushed over the edge. In such circumstances, you might react with uncharacteristic anger and do things you do not ordinarily expect of yourself.

Chronic stress tends to make aggression worse. Rather than finding yourself depressed or anxious, you might become more aggressive toward others when something annoys you. Looking at this pattern from one point of view, your aggression could be a way to protect yourself from further stress. I call this the porcupine approach to life. It keeps other people at a distance and reduces the chance that they will bother you.

However, approaching everything with anger and aggression leads you to even higher levels of stress and does not usually solve anything. Aggression can also lead you to isolation from others, conflict with people and perhaps legal entanglements.

Complications

The military, a high stress outfit especially in times of combat, has developed a number of acronyms to describe totally messed up situations including SNAFU, FUBAR and probably a few others. You can do the research about what they mean, but I think you get the idea.

In addition to depression, anxiety and aggression, you have a few other less effective choices when it comes to coping with stress or making an attempt to do so. One is social isolation. During an extended period of stress, you might conclude that it is just too hard to deal with people on a regular basis. You choose to avoid them at all costs and live life on your own terms without having to take anyone else into consideration.

Running away is another option. Teens sometimes choose this alternative literally and run away from home temporarily or for good. Adults sometimes run away from their families, jobs or other responsibilities. Ways to do this include frequently changing jobs and trading in spouses or relationship partners for new ones.

These choices often end badly with nothing resolved. Some people seek solutions to problems through random changes. They try anything new which pops into their heads with no particular plan. Without knowing what causes their stress, random changes are not likely to make much difference in their lives. They usually end up with the same problem in their new circumstances.

So, that is how your mind deals with stress. We considered the effect of stress on your body in the last chapter. Yet it affects us on other levels as well. Let's look at a couple more. Next is the world of emotions.

Life Lab Lessons

- **Do you have any of the mental signs of stress I mentioned at the beginning of this chapter?** Do they come and go or are they with you all the time? This will give you a sense of how much stress has a hold on you.

- **How well do you think under stress?** If you do okay, you are doing well managing your stress or you don't have too much of it bothering you. If you struggle to keep your wits about you in times of stress, it's time to take action.

- **Take a break from your stress.** Find a peaceful spot where you can relax and put aside your cares for a while. Go there as often as you need to and don't be in a hurry to leave.

- **What if your stress follows you to your spot?** Troubles have a way of clinging to you even when you try taking a break. One solution is to write down what is on your mind, decide when you will have time to deal with it and let it go for a while.

- **Find someone who will listen to you.** In case you have not learned this yet, you can't solve everything by yourself. Sometimes you need advice and sometimes you just need someone to hear you out.

Chapter 7- Emotions- How Do You Feel?

For peace of mind, resign as general manager of the universe.

~Author unknown~

In the last chapter, we considered how stress affects your mind. Most of the mental conditions we discussed drag your emotions along as part of the baggage. Now we will delve into the realm of emotions and feelings.

Feelings and Emotions

First, do you know the difference between an emotion and a feeling? I thought that after all my years as a psychologist I should know the answer. But when I started this chapter I realized I was not sure there was a difference. I started looking around and found interesting but conflicting opinions.

One opinion is that feelings are what you experience with your senses; emotions are how you react to your feelings physically and psychologically. Another opinion says that emotions are how you experience the world while feelings are what you make of your emotions. Not much agreement there.

Yet I did find a fair amount of agreement that you experience the world through your senses and have emotional, physical and mental reactions to what you experience. I guess that's good to know. But not all of your feelings or emotions arise from what you experience through your senses.

You might be sitting in a room minding your own business with nothing much going on around you. A memory of something troubling which occurred in the past might pop into your mind for no obvious reason and dredge up old feelings you thought you had settled.

You are capable of experiencing quite a variety of emotions/feelings. Unpleasant feelings often relate to unsettled business earlier in your life or even yesterday or today.

In reviewing chronic stress research, I found another opinion that people throughout the world share the same emotions. This is a bit hard to confirm since individuals and cultures vary in how they express their feelings.

I recently ran across a photo I took of a crowd watching acrobats performing in Key West's Mallory Square while the crowd waited for sunset. From their expressions, some people seemed amazed, some mildly amused and some indifferent. Yet I could not say for sure what any of them felt based solely on their expressions.

Some cultures value refraining from openly expressed feelings. You might have heard the term "Asian inscrutability." You learned from your family and from your culture what you should like or dislike as well as what you should fear and what you should embrace. You also learned approved ways to express how you feel and whether anyone wants to know how you feel.

As you grew older, you formed your own opinions on most matters and developed emotions to match your opinions. You might not have formed an opinion on some things which had little importance to you. You had no emotional investment in such opinions one way or another.

It looks like no one has yet won the argument about how similar emotions are across cultures or whether they are the same as feelings. Until the debate is settled and a winner announced, I will consider emotions and feelings to be what you feel in response to what you experience, either outside you or within your mind.

Initially you might be startled by a new situation and not know what to make of it. The next time you encounter this situation, you will have an easier time making sense of it as you compare it to past experience. You eventually develop a pattern of emotional response to this and similar experiences.

Too abstract? Let's try an example. Do you remember the first time you kissed someone and liked it? This can stir up quite a few emotions including sexual desire, a feeling of closeness and a desire to be even closer. It can also lead to concern about whether the other person enjoyed the kiss as much as you did, whether he or she likes you or wants to spend more time with you.

You don't always recognize your own emotions or feelings in a way you can describe. If someone asks why you are crying, you might not be able to say whether you are sad, happy or maybe a little of each. Nostalgia is a good example of such a mixed feeling, its pleasant memories mixed with regrets.

Sometimes the way you react makes it look like you are feeling one emotion when another might be closer to the truth. How about a person who says he hates gays, makes fun of them and even attacks them physically. It is possible that this person is insecure about his or her own sexuality and is acting out of fear rather than anger. One theory holds that all anger is based on fear. I'm not so sure about this one but it seems possible and even likely.

Chronic stress does not produce positive emotions but does lead to a wide variety of negative or troublesome ones. It is not always easy to know whether negative emotions cause stress, whether stress results in these emotions or whether they happen at the same time. Most of the emotions we will discuss occur after repeated or continuous exposure to particularly stressful experiences.

On first meeting with someone new, you tend to be curious unless something threatening happens or they remind you of someone you would prefer to avoid. After you get to know the person, you develop good or bad feelings about him or her depending on how your first meeting went and what happens the next few times you meet.

Your emotions generally become attached to your thoughts over a period of time, although some feelings can arise before you have a chance to think about them. If a dog chases you and bites you, it is normal to consider that dog dangerous and harmful to you. You are very likely to feel fear the next time you encounter that dog.

Thinking about your encounter can also bring back your fear, perhaps as a mild form of post traumatic stress disorder which we will consider more closely in a bit. For now let's talk a little more about fear.

Fear

You feel fear when you think you might be attacked physically or harmed in some other way. Fear sets your body and mind on high alert. With all your resources mobilized, you prepare yourself to defend against the threat or flee if it is beyond your ability to deal with it.

This is the classic fight or flight response which we touched on previously. Fear can be so strong that it paralyzes you to the point where you are unable to respond. Hopefully someone will come to your rescue at such a time.

In addition to fear of physical harm, you can fear what people might say about you, especially if you are hiding a sensitive secret. Fear can arise when you face a situation you know or imagine to be dangerous. You don't need to experience an actual attack to feel fearful. What you see in the shadows, read, watch on TV or hear from others can also arouse your fear.

Anxiety

We talked about anxiety as a thinking problem in the last chapter. It is closely related to fear. The feeling might be the same as with fear but anxiety has added features. You dwell on what happened in the past and about what might happen in the future. But you also face uncomfortable feelings in the present ranging from unease in minor situations to dread in more extreme ones. Your fear has broadened and can take on a life of its own.

Fear usually ends when the troubling event is over, while anxiety tends to linger on at least for a while. Anxiety can also attach itself to events which have not yet happened or might never happen although they might have a prominent place in your imagination. Anxiety is such a big issue that it has become a major psychiatric diagnosis with various types such as generalized anxiety disorder, panic disorder and phobia.

The American Psychiatric Association has tried to be specific about these various disorders. Generalized anxiety disorder is seen as "excessive anxiety and worry, occurring more days than not for a period of at least six months." Panic disorder is "the presence of recurrent, unexpected panic attacks followed by at least one month of persistent concern about having another panic attack." Phobia is "clinically significant anxiety." This anxiety can be attached to a specific object like a snake or a situation like public speaking. There are quite a few other classifications of anxiety disorder, but you get the idea.

After a while, you might lose track of what is making you feel anxious. You might wake up and go to bed hounded by anxiety. Perhaps the threat which led to your anxiety no longer exists. However, you have developed a state of chronic anxiety which serves no useful purpose and tends to cripple your attempts to manage your life on a daily basis. If you can't figure it out on your own and learn to deal with it, counseling would probably help.

Sweating the Small Stuff

Okay, sweating is technically something the body does. Although your mind does not perspire, I'll bet it feels like it does sometimes. First the big stuff. At its extreme, worry takes the form of a psychological disorder such as generalized anxiety disorder where your life is filled with anxiety about everything.

Another is obsessive-compulsive disorder which is based on fear that you have done or might do something wrong. You feel overcome by worry about what you did and what you are about to do. You keep doing the same things over and over hoping to get it right this time. Being consumed by this disorder allows little time for anything else and leaves you constantly exhausted.

Fortunately most people do not worry to this extent. Even if small matters look large at the moment, in the long run they turn out not to matter very much at all. For those with either of the disorders I just mentioned, self doubt comes close to paralyzing them and makes it difficult for them to quickly decide what to do in almost any situation.

Where does this feeling come from? For many people, it dates back to early childhood when they were given the impression that they were not competent to do much of anything. True, most people are not born prodigies but gradually learn survival skills and go on to develop special talents. Encouragement along the way helps them take their first faltering steps.

Have you ever watched babies learning to walk? The first awkward attempts lead nowhere except landing back on their seats. But with encouragement and support, babies are off and running before you know it.

Some parents are critical of everything their children do. Children naturally want to please their parents. But if nothing they do is acceptable, over a period of time they tend to start worrying about whether they are worthwhile or just give up trying to please their parents.

Such children grow into adults with no confidence in themselves and can start second guessing everything they do. They are not likely to take very many chances. They don't trust themselves and seldom try to develop new skills. They might also go to the other extreme and strive for perfection in everything they do. In case you haven't discovered this yet, perfection is an impossible goal to reach.

So what's the alternative? Having given up on perfection, what's left? You can do your best. Your best depends on your energy, health, mood and skills at any given time. All of these might well vary from day to day. You might not be satisfied with your best, but you can't do any better at the moment. You have given it all you've got. Perhaps you can do better at another time. But that doesn't matter. You did your best right now.

Doing your best also means being kind and gentle with yourself and being comfortable with your best efforts. It doesn't matter what others think about you. You know you did your best. Also, learn to accept others as doing their best under their current circumstances. This approach will save

73

you the trouble of worrying or fretting about things over which you have no control.

Alarm

Alarm differs from generalized anxiety in that it takes you very much by surprise. It is sudden and unanticipated. You are likely to react very strongly since you do not have time to assess what you are facing and then determine the degree of danger involved or what to do about it. With simple fear, you might have some idea what is coming and realize that you see it as threatening.

Being startled is different. You are startled by the sudden appearance of something unexpected although it might not be something all that bad for you. You just didn't see it coming, such as when your friends pop out at a surprise party. They startle you with surprise causing very brief stress which quickly leaves once you understand what is happening.

Disgust

This emotion usually results from tasting or smelling something offensive. It can also arise from reading, seeing or remembering something awful that you might have encountered in the past. People often show disgust with a scrunchy face and a feeling of nausea.

Surprisingly, at least to me, heart rate slows down as opposed to speeding up as it does with other negative emotions causing you stress. I have not been able to find a satisfactory explanation of why this is so. I guess it's just one of those odd facts.

People worldwide seem to have a built-in reaction of disgust to odors such as rotting garbage or decaying flesh. You also react with disgust to things, experiences or even ideas you encounter along your life path.

Have you ever seen the TV program *Bizarre Foods*? Just seeing some of the things people eat can turn your stomach. You might also have learned from your parents or siblings to view some foods as disgusting.

People are taught as children what tastes good and tend to accept cultural values as their own, at least initially. Would you care for some raw monkey brains? Yuck, you say? People who do like them might think butter or cow's milk is disgusting.

A reaction of disgust arrives courtesy of your senses of smell, taste, touch or hearing. In addition to sensory experiences, behaviors accepted as normal in some cultures are deemed repulsive in other cultures.

Sex between adults and teens is taboo in our culture and considered disgusting to even consider. Yet in some traditional cultures, exposure to adult sexuality or even sexual initiation by the elders is considered an appropriate way for the young to learn about sexual aspects of life. What you view as disgusting closely follows your cultural tradition whether you realize it or not.

Anger

On one recent morning in the gym locker room, I encountered a raging debate about guns. Well, not really a debate. The participants all agreed with each other. I did not hear anything rational being spoken.

Instead a diatribe about gun possession ensued with each participant trying to top the others with their outrage over a recent New York State gun control law meant to address violent crime. Everyone sounded angry, but I wondered if it was just blustering or a flexing of testosterone fueled emotions.

Anger does not come directly from experiencing or learning about a particular event. The anger comes from a combination of thoughts about a situation and feelings of great displeasure. When someone shows extreme anger, you might be tempted to tell him or her not to have a stroke. That's not bad advice since blood pressure and heart rate usually rise to match the degree of anger felt and expressed.

So why do you get angry? The closest I could come to a satisfactory answer is that anger is an emotional response to being wronged, denied or offended. In other words you are not treated the way you feel entitled to be treated. People, the weather or God may disappoint you or offend you. It does not matter whether you are entitled to what you want. You have a sense in your mind of what is right and how you should be treated. Let's look at a few examples.

Someone punches you for no good reason, at least none which makes sense to you. You have boundaries and you expect them to be respected. Being bumped crosses that boundary, punching is worse. You tell yourself this is

75

not right and respond emotionally with a feeling of anger. The amount of anger you feel depends on the degree of intrusion into your life according to how you see it.

If someone brushes against you, it is possible that you would feel a much milder emotion which you could call annoyance. If you are physically harmed, you are more likely to feel angry. This feeling could escalate to outrage. What if, after such an incident, you noticed that the person who bumped you was blind? Would you still be angry?

You also become angry when you are denied something to which you feel entitled. Lack of respect is a good example. You feel entitled to respect and become angry when you are denied that respect through what you view as prejudice.

Think about being made to sit in the back of the bus, using a separate water fountain or being barred from accommodations at a hotel because your skin is not the right color. With some historical perspective, most people learn to see such rules, formed from prejudice, as hateful. Yet prejudice and insensitivity have not vanished from our society.

Racial slurs, denigration of your sexual orientation or disparaging your national identity can send you into a tizzy. Sometimes it happens so often that you become numb and smolder inside rather than erupting in an angry outburst.

You can also become angry when people attack your religious, political or social values. Their attacks might or might not be directed personally toward you, but you could still consider them as a provocation and react as though a personal attack was intended.

Time Out for a Story

This story took place on my recent cruise to Bermuda. Once past the boarding hassle and with the ship underway, I noticed a sense of calm settling among the passengers as well as an excitement about the trip. I met six strangers at my table for dinner the first night and found all of them delightful and entertaining as was everyone else I met on the cruise.

It wasn't just my fellow passengers. I met two lifelong natives of Bermuda after we arrived in port and also a world traveler from Nottingham on the bus, although she did not know either Robin Hood or the Sheriff of Nottingham personally. All of the bar staff, waiters, cabin attendants and everyone else working on the ship shared the best of their personalities.

One evening after dinner I walked up the steps to the main concourse through the center of the ship. At the top of the stairs I came across a standoff. Two men in their thirties faced each other. Both clenched their teeth, tightened their brows, glared at each other, speaking not a word. They looked ready to tear each other apart. Fortunately, about a dozen people restrained both of them, moving them away from each other and trying to calm their respective combatants.

What started the conflict, how long it had been brewing and who initiated it all remained unclear, at least to me. All I knew was that these two individuals were at severe odds and appeared ready to attack each other. The incident appeared very incongruous in light of the camaraderie I had experienced and seen everywhere for the past few days.

Within a few moments the two groups moved the would-be fighters in separate directions with no further confrontation. The ship returned to the calm it had enjoyed just a few minutes previously. Although I never learned what the conflict was all about, I was left musing about what moves people to visible anger, especially in the midst of such a serene environment.

Anger can seethe beneath the surface and finally erupt over a seemingly minor provocation. It can also burst on the scene in response to a real or imagined wrong. The truth of the matter is not as important as how people perceive it.

I remember working in an alternative school for delinquent boys in Philadelphia. One boy would look at another and say with some contempt, "Yo' Momma!" The other boy would almost invariably raise his fists and invite the first boy to "a fair one," which meant a face-off after school if not immediately.

I can think of two things you can do to avoid such situations in your own life. One is to be aware of how your comments sound to others. The other is to give others the benefit of the doubt rather than rushing to attack them.

Hate

Anger, taken to its extreme, becomes hate which seems to consume quite of bit of energy once it starts rolling. Hate focuses on a particular situation, person or thing while anger can at times be free-floating and unattached to anything in particular.

With anger, you don't necessarily wish anyone harm. With hate, you wish the worst for the person you hate even to the point of death. Hate can be seen as an extreme form of disgust. Yet I have not heard that hate lowers your heart rate as disgust does.

Hate might mean you would choose not to have the hated object or person ever appear in your life, given a choice not to endure it. Hate can also be an all consuming feeling of revulsion fueled by anger. Terms such as loathing, abhorrence and abomination come to mind.

You often want to completely avoid the object of your hate. You could also wish the focus of your hate did not even exist. You might also take matters into our own hands, hurrying along the demise of the object of your hatred.

Then again, you might want to face a person you hate in order to spew your venom. Preoccupation with hatred fuels your stress level. Long term hatred also interferes with proceeding to more constructive activities.

Cruelty

Speaking of unproductive activity, let's consider cruelty. Cruelty is not exactly an emotion although it is an extension of hatred which we just discussed. Perhaps you find yourself tempted to dehumanize people you hate and consider them not worthy of human respect. You might even justify cruel and hurtful actions, convincing yourself that the hated person is worthy of your punishment just for existing and having the nerve to cross your path.

In addition to serving as an outlet for your hatred, cruelty can also feed a sadistic pleasure in seeing the other person suffer. I have seen cruelty and hatred follow from a feeling of being wronged by another person or by the group to which that person belongs.

It can also arise from insecurity about yourself and serve as a way for you to establish or reestablish your sense of superiority. This progression operates mostly on an emotional level with very little thought involved. Cruel people are often hard-pressed to explain their cruelty if challenged.

Sadness

Sadness is a normal feeling following the loss of someone or something dear to you. It can feel like you're weighed down with a sudden burden. Crying, loss of appetite and trouble sleeping are all quite common during periods of sadness.

Sadness relates to a specific event but is not limited to loss of things or people. You can feel sad about a failure to reach your goals or as a response to frustration that events do not turn out the way you expect, perhaps totally different from what you might expect. Sadness in itself does not usually last too long. But it can drag on into something else as we shall see.

Sorrow

Sorrow is another stress related emotion. It might start as sadness, focusing on a particular event but then continues on to a chronic state, lingering long after the loss you have suffered. The stressor usually arrives in the form of a loss, be it a loved one, a job or your health. It is possible that no one intends to upset you and there might be no one to blame.

Sorrow is a way of feeling the loss of someone or something important to you. Sometimes it is temporary and you can regain what you have lost. Other times the loss is permanent, such as the death of someone you love, and you will need to learn how to go on without the person you have lost.

You will most likely experience sorrow for some time after the death of someone close to you, usually called a period of mourning. Some people feel sorrow for a while and then try to find new relationships to replace the ones they have lost, at least to some extent. Then they find a way to get on with their lives, let go of their sorrow and hold onto their fond memories. Some people tend to wallow in their sorrow and let it consume them. They become convinced that there is no way they can go on and stay stuck indefinitely.

Often friends or relatives will try to help such a person out of the doldrums, offering advice or understanding. Sometimes that works. Sometimes it does not. Ultimately it is a choice of whether to remain stuck or find a way to get on with life.

Grieving

Elizabeth Kubler-Ross wrote about five stages of grieving in her book, *On Death and Dying*. This would be a good place to review them. She addresses the death of a loved one. Since she wrote her book, others have extended the application of her comments to other kinds of loss as well.

- **The first stage is denial.** After an unexpected death, you most likely heard at least one person, perhaps you, say, "It can't be! I just saw him last week and he seemed perfectly fine." Could it have been a mistake? Might it have been someone else? You don't want to accept it and you do whatever you can to pretend it didn't happen. Eventually you acknowledge that it did happen and you must deal with it, but how?

- **The second stage is anger.** As should be familiar to you by now, any change leads to stress. Loss of someone significant is obviously stressful. But why should you react with anger? No matter how generous a person you are, at your core you would like to have things go your way. You are angry that the person is no longer in your life. I don't see this as selfish. It's just human nature.

  Being angry about your loss is quite natural. Some people blame the person who has died, even if from natural causes. Some blame themselves or others who did not do enough to keep the deceased alive. Others blame God. Although anger is a typical reaction, most people do not remain angry indefinitely. Eventually they move on to the next stage in the process.

- **The third stage is bargaining.** This is the "If only…" stage. If only God had allowed him or her more time. If only you had been a better spouse, parent or friend. If only you lived in a different world.

  Second guessing everyone who comes to mind does not bring anyone back to life. Yet it does distract you for a while with thoughts of what might have been. Nothing changes, but it does give you a chance to reminisce about how things could have been different.

- **The fourth stage is depression.** Kubler-Ross views depression following grief more as a state of sadness than clinical depression which we discussed earlier. A stage is a waypoint toward dealing with grief rather than an endless wallowing in emotional mire.

Feeling sad is quite normal after the loss of someone who has held a prominent place in your life. How could you not miss someone who has brought joy to your life, shared your triumphs and comforted you when your life took a difficult turn?

- **Acceptance is the fifth and final stage.** You have allowed yourself to run the gamut of emotions, passing through denial, anger, bargaining and depression. You could try to avoid some of these stages. None of them are comfortable. Yet without allowing yourself to experience them, you are likely to feel unsettled from time to time. You find yourself burdened by a nagging feeling that you have work to do with your feelings about the person you have lost.

Giving yourself permission to stop for a while at each stage and taking some time to experience your feelings without harsh self-judgment will eventually bring you to acceptance. You will then be able to acknowledge your loss without being devastated by it.

You miss this person but also have many good memories you shared with him or her. You begin to recognize and appreciate what this person has brought to your life and how you have been enriched by the experience. You will be able to proceed with fond memories and a little nostalgia. You might use your good memories as a guide to how you can live your best life in the future.

Regret

Closely related to sorrow is regret. This time the sorrow is about not doing something you could have done. Or you might have done something you wish you had not done. This emotion often arises after you act, or don't act, the way you usually do or the way you would have liked to act. Others might see you in an unfavorable light or you might be disappointed in yourself for not making a better showing of yourself.

You can't undo what you did. But you can take responsibility for it and apologize to people you have hurt or offended and maybe do something to make up for what you did. This is one of the twelve steps AA relies on in dealing with alcoholism. Not coincidently, it is known as saying, "I'm sorry."

Frustration

This is another emotion which arises in combination with mental awareness. It is also akin to anger at yourself or the situation in which you find yourself. You might have spent some time developing a plan for something important in your life, perhaps a new career. You are proud of yourself for thinking of it. Finally it's time to put it into action.

Here you go. Nothing doing! It doesn't work. The stress of frustration arises when reality does not cooperate with your plan. You try another plan and that doesn't work either.

Remember earlier when we talked about lack of control as being one of the main contributors to stress? Frustration leaves you in a situation where you do not have the control you would like to have. Why can't you accomplish what you want to do? You might have heard that you can do anything you set your mind on. The sad reality is that this is not true. You can't always get what you want. Associated with frustration are feeling foolish, inept, and incompetent.

This might be a good time to mention Don Miguel Ruiz's fourth agreement for life, "Always do your best." Your best varies from time to time. What comes easily on one day might be quite a challenge on another day. You can do your best given how your body, mind, emotions and soul are functioning right now.

If this is the best you can do right now, how can you expect more of yourself? We will talk more about these agreements as we go along You can find a more complete treatment of doing your best in his book, *The Four Agreements, a Toltec Wisdom Book.*

Envy

Envy has been around forever and has a special place in the Ten Commandments. Remember the last two commandments, coveting your neighbor's goods and wife? Just because you are told not to do something doesn't mean you don't find it tempting to consider. There are two faces of envy. One is feeling bad that you don't have something or someone your neighbor has. The other is feeling bad that your neighbor has something you don't. They are two sides of the same coin, neither one very productive.

Envy might also be associated with sadness that you don't have what you want. It might include anger if you convince yourself that you deserve what someone else has. In extreme instances you might also hate your neighbor for his or her relative prosperity compared to you.

In addition to being stressful, envy is also a waste of time. Wishing your life was different does not make it so. You might also discover that what someone else has might carry its own burden which you would be better off without.

Disappointment

Disappointment is another feeling related to frustration. In this case the focus of your feeling is less on you and more on how someone else acts. In the process another person does not live up to your expectations. You react and feel as if you have a right to expect someone to act the way you want. It helps to remember that the earth does not revolve on its axis to please you. Yet this comes as a surprise to some people.

You can also focus on the weather or other events of nature which spoil your plans. It seems foolish to blame the weather for not cooperating but complaining about it seems to be a national pastime. Your time would be better spent working on how you can make the best of it and work on being flexible.

Some people take disappointment in stride and move on to the next event. Others brood on their disappointment, allowing their feelings to build to a crescendo of anger, sadness or some other overreaction. It's your choice, but there are better ways to spend your time.

Embarrassment

Embarrassment does not automatically follow an event, at least not directly. On the way to feeling embarrassed, you imagine how others would view you if they knew you did something which leaves you feeling less than proud. When you do something which does not meet your own standards or fail to do something you expect of yourself or others expect of you, feeling embarrassed often follows.

You might feel mild embarrassment when you use the wrong word in conversation. At the extreme is major embarrassment from appearing stupid in your own eyes such as when you fail at something and everyone knows it. That does not mean that it is always your fault but it can sure feel that way. There might be other emotions mixed in with embarrassment and sometimes it is difficult to know exactly what you are feeling, at least until the dust settles.

Embarrassment is not limited to feelings about your actions. You can also feel embarrassed by others' behavior, especially if you see yourself as responsible for how they act or if others associate you with them. Think of how parents feel when their children act up in public or how you might feel if a close relative of yours was convicted of a crime and sent to prison.

Shame

The feeling of shame tends to last longer than embarrassment which usually passes fairly quickly. Embarrassment usually accompanies isolated actions or situations. Shame tends to take on a life of its own and becomes part of how you view yourself over time. I remember working with a boy who had been sexually abused and was old enough to feel shame about what happened to him. During the course of treatment, I once saw him in a public setting. The look on his face was one I would imagine him to have if he was standing naked in a crowd of clothed people.

With the boy I just mentioned, his shame was not a result of his own behavior but what someone did to him. Managing misplaced blame is certainly more difficult than if you came by the blame and accompanying shame honestly, realizing that you brought it on yourself.

You might be able to think of other troubling emotions or variations on the ones we have just considered. As we have seen, people sometimes have various names for the same emotion, or feeling if you prefer, and vary in how strongly they feel these emotions as well as in the degree of stress which they experience as a result. The questions below will help you review your own emotions and feelings and apply some of what you learned to your own personal experiences.

Life Lab Lessons

- **Which of the emotions we covered in this chapter show up most in your life?** How often do these emotions take hold of you? What resources do you have for dealing with them?

- **Do you find that your feelings match the events which cause them?** Do you tend not to react with the same emotions others feel in your situation? Do you tend to overreact at times? Would you like to change anything about how strongly you react?

- **Are you able to resolve your struggle with troubling emotions fairly easily?** Or do they take hold of you and don't let you go? What can you do about that?

- **Do you have anyone to help you deal with your emotions?** We talked about some very troubling reactions and emotions. Facing them on your own might feel close to impossible. Who do you know who is willing to listen to your emotional difficulties and perhaps help you find your way out of their grip?

- **Would you like a prayer?** This is a prayer attributed to Reinhold Niebuhr and adopted by Alcoholics Anonymous. I think it can be very helpful to the rest of us as well. *Lord, grant me the strength to accept the things I cannot change, the courage to change the things I can and the wisdom to know the difference.*

Chapter 8- Spiritual Stress

God didn't do it all in one day. What makes me think I can?

~Author unknown~

If you cringe at the thought of religion and spirituality, you can skip this chapter. I would love to have you to stay, but I understand how you feel. Still you might want to try a few pages to see if there might be something here that you find useful. I wrote this book for you too and I don't want you to miss anything.

Books and articles on stress don't often address the spiritual dimension. Works that do address it tend not to combine this area with the other aspects of stress we have discussed. Yet your spirit or soul is fully capable of experiencing stress along with the rest of you. We will look at how stress and the soul are connected. We will also consider what it has to do with the stress we have already addressed which is found in other parts of you.

Spiritual or Religious

First, is there a difference between being religious and being spiritual? It depends on who you ask. For some, there is no difference. For others, there is a world of difference. I have found many definitions of spirituality as well as of religion. Both religion and spirituality center on rituals intended to bring you closer to a higher understanding of your life and its purpose.

Thomas Moore, in one of his books, has this to say about ritual, "Ritual, like art, brings imagination to the scene, which allows both participation in the event and the distance of reflection." He sees ritual as a way of reinterpreting and coming to a better sense of your life. It is possible to be spiritual while not necessarily religious. Thought of this way, atheists can also be spiritual the way I see it.

Life, Religion and Spirituality

Life is your adventure. Religion and spirituality can help you make sense of your life and navigate its challenges. When was the last time you stopped to consider what your life is all about? Why are you here on earth? Children hear that they can be anything they want to be when they grow up. That is not quite true as we have seen. Some paths require resources, money, skills or connections which might not be readily available to you. Your choices are not unlimited.

Yet you have many options readily available to you. Your family, friends, life circumstances and talents guide you toward certain paths. Those paths suggested by people who care about you might be easier follow than forging your own path although it might not take you quite where you want or expect to go. More challenging paths await you as well. These will require more effort from you since they might be less familiar although they could be more satisfying in the long run.

If fame, fortune and power are your main goals in life, you probably see little need for religion or spirituality. You will pursue your goals at all costs regardless of the effect on your life and the lives of those you encounter on your way through life. But you could end up living in a spiritual vacuum. You might want to at least think of reconsidering your priorities. Religion and spirituality are important to people who want their lives to be about something more than what they can grab for themselves. They form a context for living a life directed toward a higher calling.

When I was a child, a "vocation" was considered a call from God to pursue a higher purpose. Originally it meant being called to be a priest or a nun. Later it came to mean living any life in the context of a greater meaning.

How to find meaning outside the limited context of your little world is not always obvious. Where do you start? What are the steps? Spirituality is the process of finding, accepting and sharing the larger meaning of being alive as you journey through life. You can learn from others on a similar path to yours and share what you learn with your fellow travelers.

Religions are formalized systems intended to help you find the meaning for which you search on your spiritual journey. Obviously various religious systems cannot all be the one true path to spirituality and to God although many claim to be the only right way. Regardless of the claims, most religions start with the same purpose, living in a way which unites you with God.

How do you know if you are on the right path for you? Spirituality and religion both suggest reflection and meditation. If you never stop to see where you have been, where you are headed and the effect of your choices on you and those around you, you have no way to check your course.

Honest reflection will help you evaluate your life path to see whether it is taking you in the right direction. If you are hurting yourself or someone else as you proceed, you might have made a wrong turn and need a course correction.

Religion

Most people agree that religion is a systematic, organized set of beliefs and practices designed to bring people closer to God. Elizabeth Lesser writes, "Religions are like cookbooks and guidebooks; they suggest ingredients and point us in the right direction."

Yet religions are also institutions with expectations of their adherents, some stricter than others. Their expectations are sometimes laid on young children before they even understand what their religion is all about.

Western culture, particularly in the United States, has elevated personal progress and materialism to a kind of religion. People might attend religious services on the weekend, and then spend the rest of the week worshiping their possessions and status.

Many religious leaders and their adherents claim to have the corner on how to live and see other religions as inferior or defective. They sometimes expect to find themselves in heaven after they die but aren't so sure about followers of the "lesser" religions.

What about atheists? Someone once asked the famous atheist, George Bernard Shaw, what he would do if, when he dies, he discovers there is a God. Without missing a beat, he replied, "If, when I die I find there is a God, we shall sit down and discuss it man to man."

Religions offer a path to a relationship with God and all of them start with this noble intention. Unfortunately, over time many of them become rigid with strict boundaries for their adherents. But what about their adherents? Do they always follow along in lockstep with the doctrine and rules? At one time, most people did so. They might not have entirely agreed with what they were told but for the most part deferred to their church leaders and kept their questions and reservations to themselves.

Times are different now. At least in Western cultures, unquestioning compliance with religious tenets and rules is not as common as it once was. People now feel free to disagree with church teachings. They are not afraid to say so in their conversations and online communication. But then people are no longer burned at the stake for having their own opinions.

A poll by Univision of twelve thousand self identified Catholics in twelve countries around the world found the following:

- Sixty two percent of the respondents did not consider divorced Catholics remarried outside the church to be living in sin.

- Fifty percent thought priests should be allowed to marry.

- Forty-five percent thought women should be allowed to be priests.

- Sixty-six percent thought abortion should be allowed under at least some circumstances. Seventy-eight percent thought "artificial" contraception methods in addition to the rhythm method should be allowed.

- Thirty percent thought gay marriage was acceptable.

So it appears that the ordinary people involved, if not the religious institutions themselves, are in the process of distancing themselves from church teaching and practice. Individual priests and ministers are often more lenient in dealing with their flocks than the dogma which forms the basis of religion.

Although Pope Francis has not yet changed any church teachings, he has returned to the pastoral roots of the ancient clergy and has taken a nonjudgmental stance regarding groups of people such as Gays, divorced spouses and questioning Catholics. His approach reminds me of the way Jesus approached everyone.

Spirituality

Spirituality seems to have many often contradictory definitions. Some come close to our culture's understanding of religion while others seem to have little to do with God. They include a search for the sacred, finding a higher meaning in life, placing you in a broader context and adopting a process of life transformation. All religions encourage seeking ways to make sense of your life in a context larger than the one within the confines of your own skin.

Elizabeth Lesser described a number of critical components of spirituality found in a spiritual approach to life:

- One is fearlessness in seeking the truth about our existence.

- Another is meeting life with curiosity and openness without preconceived ideas.

- The third is accepting your life and world with wonder and happiness despite your imperfections.

- The fourth is learning to live comfortably with questions when you don't have the answers.

She sums up spirituality as approaching life with a "beginner's mind." Instead of trying to fit your life view into a rigid system of beliefs and actions, you accept your existence as an adventure which unfolds gradually and becomes more meaningful as you progress through your life.

She also suggests some ways to approach life in a spiritual way which we will consider a little later. How do all these ways of living relate to spirituality? They are all ways to transcend or go beyond your day to day life and to find a higher meaning for your existence on earth.

Manny Defines Spirituality

The very word spirituality makes some people uncomfortable. Visions may arise of monks huddled around an altar chanting in Latin. What relevance does this have to your everyday life? My life partner Carol wondered that too. She asked an addictions counselor, Manny Fortes, whom both of us knew and respected, what he thought it meant. His immediate response was, "Spirituality is being open to the goodness and joy for which you were created."

His definition seemed simple enough to me as long as you believe that you were created by God or some equivalent higher power. I did not give it much thought at first. Since she told me his definition a number of years ago, I asked her several times to remind me what he said. Finally it stuck with me.

In email correspondence with my brother about a visit to the seminary we both attended in our youth, the topic of spirituality arose. He told me he had gained his sense of spirituality in the seminary. I thought about this and realized I was too busy with my own survival as a person and the politics of the seminary to work very hard on trying to discover the meaning of spirituality which always seemed vague to me.

I was also busy trying to figure out whether I could spend the rest of my life as a priest. Later on I finally discovered the meaning of spirituality but had trouble putting it into words until I heard Manny's definition. I realized he had packed quite a bit into his brief summary. Let's look a little closer at his definition.

Being open is the first component of Manny's definition. A closed mind, or spirit, shuts off dialog with anything beyond your own little world. Your connection with the universe is broken and you have no life but that within the confines of your own body. This approach can leave you bored with your isolation, not to mention lonely. Loneliness and boredom both carry their own stress.

Being open suggests being flexible. Nothing stays the same in life. Life is always changing and plans you thought were firm sometimes have a way of not working out, at least in the way you think they should. It is necessary to look outside yourself to find a sense of greater meaning in life.

Goodness is the potential in you which lies beyond the limited world of focusing just on yourself. You have gifts unique to you which might be of benefit to perhaps one other person or maybe many people if you take the time to develop them. Anything from a smile to finding a vaccine for a major illness makes a big difference in the world. You just need to discover what you have to offer and then share it with others.

Joy is the feeling you have when you are able to find your gifts, develop them and share them with others. It is the sense of accomplishment and satisfaction coming from knowing that you are using your gifts to best advantage. I once saw a tee shirt that said, "Life's a bitch and then you die."

Life is often difficult but the point of the difficulty is not to make you suffer. You can view your suffering as a lesson you might need to learn regarding how to live this part of your life. Napoleon Hill wrote, "Inside every adversity are contained the seeds of an at least equal benefit." You can either rail against your misfortunes or open yourself to the lessons which they hold for you and use them to your advantage.

The last part of Manny's definition is "for which you were created." The point here is that you did not suddenly appear on earth by accident. Although creation remains a mystery, you were created and fit into a larger plan designed by God, Allah or whoever you refer to as your Higher Power. Within that plan you have choices to make and can be part of something much larger than yourself if you choose to. So now you know what I mean by spirituality.

If you do not believe in God or any higher power, you can still look beyond your own personal needs and desires and consider how to fit into the overall progress of the world and of humanity. What can you contribute to make life on earth a little better for others?

Stress and the Soul

Minor stressors do not usually create a religious or spiritual crisis. Yet major stressors, as we have already learned, have long term effects on the body, mind and emotions to which we can now add the life of the soul.

Your soul or spirit does not have exempt status and can be just as severely tested as the rest of you. Let's see how. If you don't think you have a soul, please accompany us anyway and see if you can find something useful in the discussion.

Life changing events often lead you to modify or at least question your values. The death of a child might steer you toward reevaluating what you find important in life. Such an experience can also lead you to question your faith and religious/spiritual beliefs.

If you were raised in a religion, you no doubt learned to see God as a loving and caring father, at least when you are behaving yourself. When you encounter the untimely loss of someone very important in your life, you will likely be tempted to wonder if God knows what he or she is doing and whether God is being fair. God's plan stinks! It sounds blasphemous, but you are still human and react with human emotions.

As you begin to understand more about life, you start to question the religious teachings with which you were raised. Reevaluating your early beliefs and teachings creates stress especially if you end up rejecting some of them as less than true or even nonsense.

You most likely found it unsettling in the past to let go of beliefs which no longer fit the values you adopted as your life progressed. Reconciling your new-found values and your old beliefs can keep you off balance until you resolve the conflicting implications for your life.

Like any other stress, spiritual stress comes in varying degrees. A little stress can distract you. Moderate stress can unnerve you. Serious chronic stress can paralyze your spiritual orientation at least for a time. Perhaps the best way to understand stress's effect on the soul is to look at an extreme case.

93

The Dark Night of the Soul

John of the Cross, a sixteenth century Carmelite mystic, coined the term "dark night of the soul." He saw it as a process of purification in which you root out all the dead wood in your life and concentrate on becoming the person God wants you to be.

Thomas Moore, in his book *Dark Nights of the Soul: a Guide to Finding Your Way through Life's Ordeals*, describes this experience as "a development which takes you away from the joy of your ordinary life."

Yet he sees dark nights as periods of transformation. Entering the dark night, it is not always clear what the transformation might involve, where you will end up or how you or others might benefit from your trial. He suggests that you use what might be a harrowing experience to make something better for your life. Here's what's involved:

- **You don't choose your dark nights.** They choose you, appearing suddenly when you least expect them. As you might have gathered, dark nights are no fun. They disrupt the ordinary course of your life but give you a chance to reevaluate where your life is headed should you choose to take it.

- **You suddenly feel buried in an avalanche of troubles.** You might be overcome by grief, wandering lost rather than proceeding merrily along your life path or feeling abandoned by someone on whom you relied deeply.

- **You might view a dark night as a state of depression.** In light of your natural haste to return to normal, you might rush to the doctor for antidepressant medication. You will most likely be tempted to get this experience behind you as quickly as possible.

By taking the easy path you will miss an opportunity. A disruption in your daily routine puts on hold your pattern of business as usual. Ordinarily you try to fit in all the activities to which you have become accustomed, perhaps being so busy that you find little time to reflect on what you are doing from minute to minute or where your life is headed in the long run.

With a break in the action, you have a chance to consider whether you are still on the path you have chosen or have wandered into the woods. The experience might also make you realize that you do not indeed have a life path but are just rambling without any clear direction.

You might not have time with your current schedule to think about your life and what course it is taking. A dark night stops you in your tracks and gives you the opportunity for self reflection. Instead of viewing your predicament as a tragedy and feeling sorry for yourself, you now have a chance to make a course correction in your life if needed.

You might learn that you are doing fairly well staying on the course you have set for yourself. Or you could discover that you have forgotten how you wanted to live your life. At the very least you might discover that you do not have the most effective ways of coping with misfortune and its stress.

Maybe this is your first major disaster and you have no idea what to do about it. Now is the time to discover who you can count on when you are in trouble. It's also a time to learn some new skills you can use to cope with future life challenges.

It seems to me that minor spiritual crises are lesser varieties of the dark night we are considering. Although not protracted periods of self searching, these crises also offer you an opportunity to reexamine your approach to life should you choose to accept the challenge.

In my opinion, the nature of life is that people are either growing or dying. This applies to your soul as well as to your body. You don't look forward to the trials awaiting you during the course of your life. Yet they offer you the chance to refine your approach to life as the smelter does with precious metal ore. You can gain something precious from your challenge if you have the patience and courage to see it through.

Life Lab Lessons

- **What does spirituality mean to you?** Do you see any meaning in your life beyond your own survival? Whether or not your follow a religious practice, you can always find a larger meaning for your life.

- **If you are a member of a particular religion, does it help you live a better life than you would without it?** If you answer yes, be grateful and keep doing what you are doing. If not, you might want to consider what you can change about the meaning of your religion in your life. Another possibility would be to find a religion closer fitting your personal goals.

- **How do you see spirituality as it relates to your life?** We just looked at several ways to incorporate spirituality into your life. Perhaps you have already figured this out for yourself or maybe one of the ways we looked at will make sense to you.

95

- **What questions do you have about religion and spirituality?** You are an adult now and it is okay to question what you have believed and practiced for years. You might need to make changes in how you view your relationship with God and the universe. It's okay to wonder and to experiment.

- **Have you experienced a dark night of the soul?** Most people do at one point or another. Perhaps you are in one right now. Obviously, it is no picnic. I hope that from what I said, you will learn from it valuable lessons for your life in the future.

Chapter 9- The Joy of Stress

Doing something that is productive is a great way to alleviate stress.
Get your mind doing something productive.

~Ziggy Marley~

I'll bet you didn't expect to find a chapter like this. Most of what we have seen so far about stress is that it's, well, stressful. In your struggles with stress to right yourself and the world you live in, you may tend to see everything that happens to you as a challenge. You saw in the previous chapter that even extreme trials of the soul can be turned into something useful in your life. Sometimes stress does not need to be quite such a burden but can still be a positive force in your life as well as a trial.

I am not suggesting that stress is fun. It isn't. In previous chapters we looked at the many ways stress finds its way into your life and the negative effects it has on every part of you. Yet the outcomes of some stressful experiences can be rewarding. That is the focus of this chapter.

The question you have to ask yourself is whether it's worth taking on stress when you have a choice. There is no right or wrong answer. Yet your answer determines what kind of life you will have. In chapter four we looked at stress you choose as a part of challenges you accept for yourself. Here we will take a closer look at self chosen stress which has at least the promise of a good outcome for you.

Growing Up

Do you really have any choice about growing up? At first blush, it looks like you don't. You had no say in the choice to bring you onto the planet. Your task is to grow up whether you want to or not.

Growing up often means letting go of the carefree existence you might have had as a child. Of course not all children are carefree, but even children raised in what you might consider dreadful circumstances still find a way to engage in play of one kind or another. They exist in a magical world of make believe like everybody else at least some of the time, reincarnations of Peter Pan in Neverland.

97

The Bible speaks of adulthood as a time of putting away the things of a child. I'm not sure you need to put them away permanently. Maybe they should just go on the shelf for a time while you get on with the serious business of living and save play for a little later.

Growing up is certainly more stressful than remaining a child. It involves making decisions about where your life is headed, taking responsibility for what you do and don't do as well as accepting the consequences of your actions.

That sounds stressful to me. How about you? Crossing the border between childhood and adulthood, you have a chance to take responsibility for your life for the first time. What if you choose unwisely and make poor decisions?

What if you are unsuccessful in reaching your goals? For you, growing up now means taking risks and venturing into the unknown. You are now responsible for your own life and have no one else to blame if things turn out poorly. It's also up to you to change direction if you don't like the one in which you are headed.

Before we talk more about growing up, let's consider the alternative. If you choose not to grow up and make a life for yourself, you may be left to take the dregs others leave for you and have no say in how your life turns out. In some ways this is a safer route.

No one can blame you for making mistakes if you choose not to accept any challenges or to decide anything for yourself. Maybe you can find someone to take care of you and take responsibility for you or you can rely on welfare programs while you eke out a subsistence living. But what will you have to show for it in the long run?

If you were fortunate enough to have a childhood where you were supported and encouraged to take little chances, baby steps if you will, you can learn to trust yourself to start making more important choices. They may not all be good ones.

I don't know anyone who has made good choices every time. Everybody makes mistakes. Sometimes you might imagine that life is easy for others while you struggle. If you switched places with someone else for a week, you might not still think so.

Some people stop choosing for themselves, leaving control of their lives to someone else, while others learn from their mistakes and eventually make better decisions. This is an opportunity to find out what does and does not work for you. Succeeding in this choice brings you joy.

Your plan might have turned out to be a failure but that doesn't mean that you are a failure. At least you can chalk it up to experience, learn from your failures and focus on more promising plans in the future.

Eventually succeeding with small risks, you will begin to trust yourself to make more weighty decisions and eventually find a life path which brings you joy, peace and satisfaction. Even then you are not necessarily out of the woods.

Many millionaires have lost and gained fortunes repeatedly. Hopefully you will have enough self confidence to get up when you stumble, learn from your experience and continue along your path toward realizing your potential.

Academic Achievement

For some students, getting good grades is easy. All they have to do is show up and pay a reasonable amount of attention in school. Not much stress there. For others, from grammar school through graduate school, getting good grades is a constant challenge. Even average marks might come with great difficulty.

You can avoid this stress by not trying very hard. But then there is the risk of being considered a dummy and ending up without any worthwhile life skills.

For those who struggle, trying to get good grades is a risk. What if you try your best and still end up with poor grades? The stress of failure weighs on you, at least until you find a new plan that makes you happy.

Some people must make difficult choices. Maybe you need to choose between academics, sports and social life and don't have the resources or capabilities to excel in all three areas. You also risk the possibility of not doing as well as you would like to in any of these areas. But if you do succeed, even if in only one area, you often feel better about yourself and see the stress and sacrifice as worthwhile.

Work

Regardless of how you do in school, finding work can be stressful as well. Even if you are well prepared academically for the work you choose, much of what is expected on the job is not taught in school. New relationships await you as well as the new expectations of the job itself and the culture in the company for which you will work.

You might be required to change your wardrobe, the way you eat and your daily schedule. What you do all day will be evaluated and judged by your boss. Sometimes bosses are not very good at conveying their expectations. I know of more than one person with several supervisors laying down conflicting expectations for how they should conduct themselves at work. No matter what they do, they please one supervisor and annoy the others. Time for a new job?

The social climate at work might also become a challenge. Coworkers might have expectations of you which don't match your values or ethics and might also differ from management expectations.

Learning to negotiate the labyrinth of varying or even conflicting work expectations can be quite stressful, but worth it in the end if you can master it and prosper as a result. Even if your new job does not work out, eventually your experience will prepare you to more easily face the challenges of your next job.

Work Advancement

Promotions at work present their own challenges along with the benefits. Former colleagues on your level might be jealous of your promotion. You will most likely face a new set of expectations for the quantity and quality of work you will do. You might now have responsibility for the performance of your former colleagues. You will need to stay aware of these shifting relationships and find a way to manage them.

Your new responsibilities usually affect your home life or social activities as well. You might need to adapt to others' expectations of you and deal with their reactions to your promotion. This is all part and parcel of moving up the ladder and pay scale at work. You can also learn how to balance your work life with your home life.

Marriage

We talked about the possible stresses associated with marriage and similar relationships in Chapter 4. You choose marriage but you do not always knowingly choose the stress which accompanies it. Yet stress follows as part of the deal at some point. Many people are still in the dream world or gaga stage when they marry and haven't given much thought to the challenges marriage can present.

Now you no longer have just yourself to think about. Most married couples live together. When they were single, they might have had very different ways of keeping house, shopping, eating, spending their free time, finding ways to relax and socialize.

All these activities and more will require adapting to shared space as well as reconciling differing values and priorities with another person. A harmonious marriage makes navigating these differences worthwhile. Not navigating them just increases stress. The same applies to the increasing number of committed relationships not involving formal marriage.

Children

Children can be a blessing and a joy but they don't come without their own challenges any more than marriage does. If you look closely at your own childhood, you will realize that you created a challenge for your parents whether you wanted to or not. Illness, school difficulties and your mistakes as you learned how to be more responsible. All these took a toll on your parents.

Don't expect raising your own children to be any different. Parents often get stuck and wish their children came with an instruction manual. What to do now? There is no foolproof manual for raising children because each child is unique.

Some children are very easy to raise and others present a constant challenge. No two children present quite the same challenges either. If you stick with it, the reward of seeing your children leave the nest to live successful lives is well worth the effort.

Technology

Life was once simpler if not less stressful. Over recent decades, life has become cluttered by increasing technology or perhaps made easier, depending on your point of view. Three year olds these days seem more comfortable with computers than their grandparents or even their parents.

101

Many adults find themselves overwhelmed by the changing demands of technology.

One interesting development is the effect on communication. Today you can be in touch with others around the world instantaneously. You can document and share even the smallest events of your daily life through your phone and almost everything you do from moment to moment might become the subject of a text message.

While you are in immediate contact with others, has this really improved your communication? Immediacy makes it more difficult to think about what you want to say to others and, at least in my opinion, makes meaningful communication more difficult. I would venture to say that the majority of text messages are of little consequence.

I remember when my brother and I had a misunderstanding. Because of time zone differences and different work schedules, we found it hard to find a mutually convenient time to talk with each other on the phone. We tried to resolve the issue by email.

Each time we tried to clarify the issue, our emotional distance increased. I eventually realized that technology had blocked our emotions from our communication. The words might have gotten through but what we meant and how we felt did not.

While technology might make your communication easier and faster, it does not necessarily improve it. Take care how you communicate in order to avoid placing more stress on your relationships which can be fragile at times. Use technology as a tool rather than a god.

The Arts

We will look later at the arts as a way to approach stress. Now let's consider stress as part of the bargain for artistic creativity. Most artists turn to art because they have something to say. It might be a way to sort out how they feel about themselves or to share their perceptions, thoughts and emotions with the rest of the world.

In 1963, I reluctantly began the study of Scholastic Philosophy as set out by Thomas Aquinas. This thirteenth century Dominican monk interpreted what Aristotle had to say on various philosophical topics. He also suggested ways of understanding the world and our experiences in it. I still remember how Aquinas defined art as "right reason about something to be made." That made about as little sense to me as did the rest of his writings.

I reviewed his comments recently to see if I had been overly harsh in my judgment of him. In the process I ran across his statement, "A man who works with his hands is a laborer; a man who works with his hands and his mind is a craftsman; a man who works with his hands and his brain and his heart is an artist." Finally I had discovered a bit of Thomistic thinking which made sense to me.

After reading a newspaper column a while ago about "bad art," I puzzled about what that meant. Do I believe in such a thing? I finally concluded that some art does not follow the conventions of the genre of art in which the artist works. Being different does not necessarily mean creating bad art. Some artists are not appreciated until well after they die.

I recall a recent conversation with an artist at an outdoor art exhibit. Viewing his work gave me a sense of joy and peace. I asked if he had considered exhibiting on a larger scale. He looked surprised. After a little discussion, the truth came out. Standing amid his paintings in a tent out in the country, he admitted that he wasn't sure his art was good enough for a gallery.

So what makes art good enough? When first exposed to art materials, children produce wonderful images of how the world looks to them. As they are taught the "rules" of art, their spontaneity often gets squashed and they revert to the safety of what we think of as childish art.

Critics have standards by which they judge the quality of art. Galleries have standards for what they will display. Patrons like some art works, pass by others with indifference and frown at still others. Critics, galleries and patrons often disagree among themselves and with each other about what art is and what makes it good or bad.

When I worked at an arts council a while back, I started asking artists why they do what they do. One artist said she uses her art to express her emotions in a therapeutic way. Another artist uses his photographs to show people what is out there in nature.

There are probably as many motivations for producing art as there are artists. It's up to each of us to decide what art is and whether it's "good" or "bad." Other viewers and critics can decide for themselves what they like.

In any case, those who encounter art will make judgments about it, for better or worse. Artists sometimes receive recognition and feel appreciated. Others feel rejected as have many great artists and musicians over the years and only come to be appreciated long after they're gone. There is joy in being recognized. Some artists make do with the satisfaction of representing what is in their minds.

The Pen and the Stage

So far here we have been talking about fine art. The same risks and associated stress accompany writers and performers of all sorts. They put themselves on the line when they produce their work and share it.

The form of stress varies from one artist to another. You have no doubt heard of stage fright which many performers experience as they approach each performance. Performing artists and public speakers on stage are in full view every moment. If they trip, miss a note or forget their lines, it is immediately obvious to the trained observer and sometimes to the not so trained one.

Writers have a little more leeway. They can edit what they write, decide not to publish their work or seek help revising it before offering to the public. Once their writing is made public, they are subject to the same public scrutiny as performers.

Yet they are judged only on the merits of their writing and not on their public performance of it. So their experience with public criticism might be a little less stressful.

Regardless of how their appearance and presentation are received, writers and public speakers are also judged on the content or their work, while performers often portray work written or composed up by someone else.

And All the Rest

We have considered a few examples of the risks people take on, the stress which results and the benefits they hope to receive from their risk. No doubt you can think of other stressors you or those you know have accepted as part of life to accomplish something important. How much stress you are willing to endure depends on how important your goals are to you.

Life Lab Lessons

- **Did you know stress had a positive side?** Looking at it this way goes along with the way you look at everything else in life. Some see the advantages and some the disadvantages. Seeing the bright side makes stress a little easier to manage.

- **Try listing what you have accomplished in your life so far by taking a chance and absorbing stress in the process.** You might be surprised how much you can accomplish when you put your mind to it. When you look at your stress along with what you have accomplished, the stress might not look like quite so much of a burden.

- **Do you see technology as a stress reliever or another stressful burden in your life?** It can be both at the same time. I think it is important for you to keep it in perspective and not let it become the most important thing in your life so that your gadgets take over life.

- **What artistic talents do you have?** You don't need to become a professional artist along with the stress that goes along with it. Art can be a way of relaxing or of expressing your opinions or feelings on any aspect of your life even if just for your own satisfaction.

- **Look at the cost of stress.** When planning a project or activity, consider what stress might come with it. Then decide if it is worth it to you or not. It's a lot like budgeting your money.

Chapter 10- Avoiding Stress

Stress is an ignorant state.
It believes that everything is an emergency.

~Natalie Goldberg~

So far, I have reviewed with you the many stressors which find you or which you accept willingly. We have also seen how stress affects you on various levels. Maybe you were anxious to see what you can do about your stress and jumped to this chapter right away. In any case, I'm glad you are still with me. Let's get on with our journey.

There is no one best way to deal with stress. One approach is to try avoiding it altogether. If you manage an end run and avoid stress in the first place, then you can relax. Unfortunately this is easier said than done. It might work sometimes with the choices and related stress you invite into your life. You can forego the stress and pursue the possibilities for accomplishment. But, as you have seen, many stressors sneak up on you and these are harder to avoid.

Another possibility is to face your stress head on, understanding how it affects you. Then you can make changes in your life to eliminate or reduce it. Sometimes stress feels overwhelming. If it seems too much to manage, you might just accept it and try to live with it the best you can.

If you are a fighter, you can go toe to toe with stress in an attempt to push it out of your life. To take this approach, you need enough faith in yourself to enter the ring. You will see more about taking on stress head-on in the next chapter.

A third possibility is to transform or reframe your stress. You can learn to see your stress in a different light from when you first faced it. You had a taste of how this is done a little earlier when I discussed the dark night of the soul. More about this in Chapter 12.

Stop Spinning Your Wheels

In this chapter, we will look at how to avoid stress or at least minimize it. Remember when I talked about lack of control and uncertainty being key contributors to stress. Here they are again. It is hard to get control of your life if you don't know where it's headed.

The philosopher Martin Heidegger talked about three levels of awareness in life. The first is awareness of your own concerns and activities. I will spare you his German words.

At this level, you are concerned only about what happens in your own little world. You have no idea what is happening in the society which surrounds you or in the rest of the world. You sit on a log or wander around in circles. You don't know what to do with your life because it has no context. We talked about this a little in the chapter on spirituality.

The second level of awareness is being in touch with the world including your place in it and the place of other people as well. At this level you are more aware of what is going on around you even if at a somewhat superficial level. You see what is happening but don't stop to ponder what it all means.

The third level is hard to translate meaningfully from the German. The closest I can come to its meaning in English is awareness with the ability to reflect on your situation. My understanding of this level is that you are fully aware of your inner workings and surroundings. You understand your thoughts and feelings as well as how they relate to the universe and human environment around you.

Moving up through these three levels, you come to a better understanding of life and what it means to you. At the highest level of understanding, it is time for you to decide what your life means and what you want to get from it as well as what you have to share with others. I consider this the same as knowing your purpose in life.

You don't reach this level of understanding overnight. As a child you had daydreams about what you wanted to do with your life but they were subject to change at a moment's notice whenever a new possibility popped into your head. During adolescence or early adulthood, most people come to at least an initial understanding of what they want their lives to be about.

Once you have this in mind, you can tailor your education and job experience to help you finalize your goals and get on with them for the foreseeable future. As I mentioned earlier, people often switch paths several times during the course of their lives, sometimes heading in directions they never imagined. When I started work as a psychologist, I never imagined working at an arts council or writing articles and books.

Perhaps you will stay on the same life path throughout your life, gradually developing and deepening your goals and adding to your accomplishments. On the other hand, at some point in your life you might find yourself doing something completely different from what you had originally planned. Dramatic changes can take place several times throughout your life.

The average person has at least three different careers during a lifetime. If you make such changes, your unique set of skills might come in handy but you will probably need to develop new ones as well. Although the changes will be stressful, they might lead to a less stressful lifestyle in the long run.

Look in the Lifestyle Mirror

Once you have settled on a way of life, at least for the time being, you adopt a normal routine for each day, geared toward achieving your life goals. If you have thoroughly considered where you are headed, you probably choose your daily activities carefully to match your goals. Finding a routine you can live with keeps you from waking up each morning and wondering what your life is all about.

When you start down a new path, you have no way to know for sure whether you are taking the right steps to get where you want to be. Perhaps you will need advice from those who want to help you or you may read about how to achieve what you want.

The only way to know for sure if this is the right path for you is to take time out once in a while to review your life so far and see whether it is bringing you closer to where you want to be. If not, it is time to consider some course corrections. This might involve new research as well as further trial and error. Plato said, "The unexamined life is not worth living." I believe this is what he meant.

Always Do Your Best

Most people have standards for themselves and their behavior in terms of the goals they have for their lives. If your goal is perfection, you are setting yourself up for stress and disappointment, since no one reaches perfection in life no matter how hard they try. There is always room for improvement.

A better goal would be one suggested by Don Miguel Ruiz which I mentioned a little earlier, Let me elaborate. We are looking here at his fourth agreement, "Always do your best." When I first read this agreement, it seemed impossible. I thought of the times I felt I was doing my best: first learning to water ski, the oral examination for my doctorate and the endurance test to qualify as a soccer referee. I felt exhausted after each of these efforts and knew I could not keep up the pace for very long. How could I do this all the time?

I read further in Ruiz's book that doing your best means the best you can do with the resources you have available in your present circumstances. Your best varies from task to task. Your best will be much better doing something you are proficient in than doing something you are just learning. Your best will also be better when you are healthy, rested and focused than it is when you are sick, exhausted or distracted. Your best is not always the same but changes all the time. This seems more manageable than trying to be perfect.

Doing your best means pacing yourself by not trying to do more than is possible for you to do. Overexerting yourself would quickly exhaust or discourage you and either slow you down or prevent you from reaching your goals altogether.

Doing your best also means actually doing something. Having good intentions is not enough. Telling yourself you will get more exercise or eat better does not make you any healthier. It only makes a difference if you follow through on your intentions and do what you have been planning.

But it is not enough to take action. You can only do your best when you love what you are doing. If you are doing something because someone else wants you to or because you will be paid for it or rewarded in some other way, it will probably not be your best. You have to be enthusiastic about what you are doing in order to use all your resources.

Doing your best also means accepting yourself as you are, with the skills you have now and with your current level of functioning. Wishing you could do better distracts you from doing the best you can right now and only serves to discourage you by making you think how things could be better under different circumstances.

This is not to say that you can't learn from your mistakes. You can improve your skills or find a way to change your circumstances so that the next time your best can be better than it is right now.

You also need to remember that you are here on earth to live, be happy and love. If you stay focused on these three goals, you will be the best you can be at each moment, with the abilities you have and in your current circumstances. You can live with that and rest easy when the time comes to look back on how you did.

Know What You Want and Who Supports You

Once you have settled on your goals and started to pursue them, it would be helpful to know who is on your team. Trying to reach your goals in a vacuum can quickly become a frustrating experience and provides more stress too.

If you discover your passion when you are young, you have time to find your own path. You follow many other people who have discovered their passions or set about to make pursuing them their life work. Many people have gone before you and have already made their own mistakes and learned from them. Instead of starting from scratch, you can learn by others' example and save yourself quite a bit of trouble.

Sometimes you can learn from books written about journeys others have taken. They can often provide hints and advice about how they overcame obstacles and learned to find success. Their experience might help guide you along your own path.

One of your friends may be in the same boat as you or know someone who can be helpful to you on your journey. Don't be afraid to ask for help. That does not mean you need to follow exactly in someone else's footsteps but it could make life easier for you and reduce your stress in the process.

Actually, you can't follow precisely in someone else's footsteps. Your path is unique. But you might learn from their mistakes and save yourself some trouble and frustration. Becoming familiar with someone else's journey might also give you some ideas you have not considered for your own journey. It might also help you stay focused on your path or find a new focus if your current path turns out not to be the right one for you.

No matter what you decide to do with your life, my guess is that you will find some people agree with your decision and others will think it foolish. When I decided to enter the seminary at age thirteen, I got quite a bit of support from my rather religious family. Two years later, my grandfather told me that I had gone to the seminary at too young an age. He might have had a point, but it was not of much help two years after I had already made my decision.

Why do home teams often do better in sports than visiting teams? They're in familiar territory and also have many more fans cheering them on than the visiting team. The more supporters you have the better you will feel about your major decisions and how you go about implementing them.

What about your critics? Should you just write them off? I wouldn't be so quick to do so. They usually see the pitfalls lying ahead of you. Although you are more likely to listen to your supporters, your detractors might have valid points as well. Listening to their cautions can save you lots of anxiety. You don't have to give up your dreams but it never hurts to be a little careful and watch your step to be sure you stay on the right path.

Staying in a Relationship

Finding support for your goals is important in reducing stress. For many people, their main support comes from the person to whom they are married or a partner with whom they share a long term relationship.

When I first worked with couples, I thought the key to a better relationship was good communication. As my career continued, I realized that marriage and similar relationships were more complicated than that. I also learned that there is no easy solution to staying together. Half of all marriages last and half don't, despite a commitment "until death do us part." I have not encountered any reliable statistics on the comparative success rate of relationships outside of marriage but I would guess it is similar to marriage.

Most people say they got together because they loved each other. But what does that mean? Love can include sexual or romantic feelings, finding someone who cares about you or a person you care about. Maybe you are just comfortable with that person.

Many potential partners look for someone to take care of them. They may also be in the market for someone to take care of. It is very easy to fall into the trap of depending on someone who might not always be there or trying to control the other person to keep the relationship the way you want it to be.

What does it take to keep the commitment alive? In his book, *Passionate Marriage*, David Schnarch suggests that one of the most important tasks is for each spouse or partner is to know himself or herself before entering into a commitment.

If you don't know what you want from life, how can you reasonably expect another person to share your life with you and help you pursue your goals? What are you asking the other person to share?

Let's assume that two people understand what they want from life, share their goals with each other and agree to support each other in attaining them. That's a good start. But wait a minute. Think back to how your life was ten, twenty or thirty years ago and what was important to you back then. Have you changed?

Most of us are quite different now than we were in the past. If you are in a long term relationship, think back to what you were like when you met. There is no way to predict with any certainty what you will be like in the future or what your partner will be like.

Your chances of staying together improve greatly if you both enter your relationship with a sense of adventure rather than with definite ideas about how the relationship should start and remain in the future. You are setting out on an unknown voyage. Life circumstances, finances and health might alter your voyage considerably.

You or your partner or both might discover new life destinations. Perhaps you will learn new ways to approach life, taking you in different directions than you agreed on when your relationship began, if indeed you had such a conversation.

It will take a great deal of flexibility from both of you to weather all the challenges and surprises life has in store for you. To be successful, you must be responsible for meeting your own goals and support your partner in reaching his or her goals. This is also the best way to minimize stress in your relationship.

What Is Important?

This is where you start getting organized. Once you have an idea where you want to go in life and have some independent goals or perhaps ideas you have gathered from others, where do you start? Having your target goal in mind gives you a general plan for how to proceed. But then what?

You can amble along at random, trying one thing after another to see what works. We just discussed looking to others for support and also for necessary cautions which might not occur to you on your own. Still, this is your journey and what you end up doing about it is still your choice.

What about a roadmap? If you going on a trip you have never taken before, would you jump in the car and just start driving, hoping you will arrive at your destination? How stressful would that be? So, how about a roadmap to reach your goals? Now that you are clear where you want to be, you have a few things to consider:

- What resources do you need to take with you on your journey?

- You will most likely need certain skills which you can learn from formal study in a field related to your chosen profession or from others who already have the skills you need.

113

- You might need to pay your dues and work your way up to where you would like to be.

- Depending on what your goals are, you may need to gain some experience along the way. What steps will you take? We've already talked about consulting others who have taken paths similar to yours.

- Having a mentor or coach gets you started and also moves you along your path more quickly than you probably would be able to do on your own.

- Rather than relying on intuition with no real plan, consider putting your goals in writing and also writing down how you will know if you are being successful or not. Learn what success will look like to you when you have accomplished your goal.

- You may not know for sure what steps to take, even with guidance, especially if you have chosen a unique path. Keeping written track of your progress is a good way to see what works and what does not and also to make sure you are getting closer to where you want to be over time.

Minimize Stress along Your Path

It would be nice if you could set up a completely stress free life. Or at least it seems that way. But as we saw in the last chapter, a little stress can be a good thing. Without it you would not have much motivation to get yourself in gear to do something constructive. Did you know that people under moderate stress do better on most tasks than those with very little or too much stress? Stress can alert you along your chosen path to dangers you encounter and also remind you when you need to make adjustments.

It is possible to minimize the amount of stress you encounter. As we have seen, you don't have much choice about the stress which finds you during the ordinary course of life. But we also saw that there are plenty of times when you choose stress for various reasons. By considering your life over a period of time, you can see your pattern of choosing stress and whether you made good choices.

You can look back over your stress-laden choices and decide whether or not they have worked to your advantage. If not, you always have the option of doing something different next time. You remember the definition of craziness don't you? That's when you keep doing the same thing over and over and expect a different result.

Add It to Your List

Have you ever gotten to the end of the day and realized you forgot to do something important. We all have. You start with good intentions and might get most of your tasks done. But without some organization, what you actually accomplish might be quite important, trivial or somewhere in between.

Here are a few things to remember to make your lists more useful:

- If you only have a few things to do on a given day, it might not be difficult to get everything done.

- If you have many things to do, making a list should help you see what lies ahead for the day.

- Once everything is on your list, the next step is to rank the tasks by importance. Getting all the little things done is not much consolation if you overlook something critical.

- Starting at the top with the most important tasks will help you prioritize your time.

- As you look over your list, you might realize that you will not have to do everything on it.

- You can put off some of the less important tasks for another day.

- If you still don't have time to do everything important, perhaps someone else can do one or two things for you.

- You could also make your apologies to someone expecting something of you and reschedule a better time to attend to his or her needs.

All this takes time but it is certainly better than letting someone down and trying to make amends later. In the long run, it is less stressful as well.

Finish What You Start

Loose ends can trip you up. Let's say you began your day with five projects and started working on all of them sometime during the day but finish none of them. How might that cause stress? You will have no sense of accomplishment about completing even one project.

If you do decide to return to one of them, how will you remember where you were with the others when you return to them? You can end up spending more time finding your place and remembering what you were trying to do than actually doing anything.

Doing several things at once blunts your attention. You can't give them all equal attention or expect to do a good job on tasks which get only part of your attention and energy. You will be looking back to the past and ahead to the future while only partially focusing on the present. You would do better to prioritize your tasks, start with the most important one and finish it before moving on. Try it and see if this works for you.

Save Yourself Some Free Time

When was the last time something you set out to accomplish took exactly the amount of time you expected it to? If you have more things planned than you can reasonably be expected to complete, you will most likely rush through them, not doing as well as you might have.

You might complete everything on your list but end up cutting corners to get everything done. If you take your time, you might accomplish some of your goals but leave others undone. This is okay if you have set priorities and get the important things done.

One way to avoid this problem is to build some free time into your schedule. This way you allow for jobs taking longer than you expected. You might even have some time for a little fun when you are finished working on your priorities.

Be Kind to Yourself

You are in the best position to know what you need and want. If you don't know, spend some time listening to your mind and getting in touch with your feelings. This would also be a good time to check in with your soul and revisit the meaning of your life. Life is a constant series of choices. Some of them are in your best interest. With some others, you can shoot yourself in the foot if you are not careful.

Tracking your choices, perhaps with a journal, helps you document how well your choices work out for you. If you keep making the wrong choices with the same negative results, there is probably a reason why. Paying attention to your pattern should give you some idea why you keep getting stuck in the same rut. It should also give you some incentive to make changes so you can act in your own best interest more consistently.

Pony Express and Stage Coach

Many people are constantly on the go from dawn to midnight. Even if you learn to manage your schedule well and get everything done, it still may feel like you have no time left for yourself. Exhaustion and its attendant stress soon catch up to you in this mode.

Some people think only of their own relaxation and don't get much done. Others race through the day trying to keep everyone happy. As a happy medium, you learn to do what is important while also saving some relaxation time for yourself.

Some people don't know how to relax. Others might think it is selfish to focus on their own comfort. Do you remember the pony express and stage coaches? Well, you probably don't remember them but surely you have heard stories about them even if they have not ridden by your house lately.

The ponies traveled about ten miles between stations where the rider switched mounts and took off again. Riders usually traveled about seventy-five miles or so before new ones took their place.

I visited a restaurant not too far from my home which was once a stage coach stop. I learned that the horses were unhitched after a certain number of miles, the distance being known as a stage. Dinner was served, and a new team of horses put in the harness for the next stage.

If they didn't change horses, the whole venture would grind to a halt before too long. You don't have any more stamina than a horse, probably much less. You need to stop for rest every so often in order to be ready to continue your journey. Maybe your life is not as grueling as those of the pony express riders and stage coach drivers. But you don't have unlimited endurance. Even during very routine work, you tend to lose focus and concentration on what you are doing without some breaks for rest.

The more boring the work, the harder it is to keep your focus. Very demanding work can also wear you down after a while. It's not a question of whether you would like to rest. It is a necessity in order to stay effective.

Do What You Enjoy

Relaxing does not always mean doing nothing, although it might at times. Sometimes you will want to just lie in bed or in a lounge chair without turning on your mind or body. After a while you will most likely become restless and need to get up to do something. Jumping right back into the daily grind immediately does not help with your relaxation. Enjoy the calm.

That's what hobbies are for, as well as time with friends, walking in the woods, sitting on a beach watching the waves or viewing sports where the outcome of the game is not critical to your wellbeing.

You might also indulge in the arts whether it is painting, drawing or pottery. Time with friends, your spouse or partner, and social events of all sorts, reading and listening to music also count, although you don't have to keep score.

My brothers and I play Zen golf every few years. There's no rush. We start on any hole which seems interesting. We play until we feel like stopping, whether or not we have finished all the holes. And we don't keep score.

Most likely you have certain activities you find relaxing, assuming you give yourself the time. If you don't know what you would like to do, experiment. Most weekend editions of local newspapers are full of activities some of which might interest you. Try something you have never done before. Maybe you will discover something you really like and perhaps develop a new hobby.

Keep Your Sense of Humor

Sometimes people take life too seriously and feel a need to make every second count with fierce determination. Yet you are surrounded by silliness, your own and that of other people, which can evoke a smile or even a belly laugh if you lighten up for a little while.

You don't need to wait until you are embroiled in stress to have some fun. Waiting that long can make it difficult to switch gears. Researchers at the Mayo Clinic noted that in the short term, humor generates endorphins, stimulates many of your organs and activates them. It also calms down your stress response including heart rate and blood pressure, and soothes tension by stimulating circulation and muscle relaxation.

In the long run, humor improves your immune system by releasing chemicals which fight stress and illness and relieves pain by releasing natural pain killers. Humor increases personal satisfaction making it easier to cope with difficult situations and improves your mood by lessening depression and anxiety and making you feel happier. Sounds like a good prescription to me. No copay either!

Eat Healthy

We have spent most of this chapter seeing how you can ward off stress by tending to your mind and emotions. Your body can help insulate you from stress as well. Here's how. What you eat can take a toll on your body and make it harder for you to find the energy to deal with stressful situations.

For years our culture has drifted toward food and quasi-food that is quick, easy and good tasting. These foods or food like substances appeal more to immediate pleasure than to good nutrition which fortifies you for life's challenges. They are known as comfort foods, like macaroni and cheese, fried chicken and ice cream.

Your own favorites make you feel good for the moment. When you concentrate only on feeling good you might ignore nutrition and not do your body any favors. You can also increase your chances of chronic disease with poor food choices which in turn add to chronic stress.

There are plenty of foods which help prepare you to combat and limit the effect of stress on your body. In case you want to experiment, here are a few:

- asparagus
- avocados
- berries

119

- cashews

- chamomile tea

- chocolate

- garlic

- grass-fed beef

- green tea

- oatmeal

- oranges

- oysters

- walnuts

Give them a try. Your body will thank you. You can also experiment with other foods to see what effect they have on you and your stress level. Pay close attention and you will begin to notice what makes you feel better or worse.

Get Moving

It might seem like a contradiction, but exercise is a great way to relax. What does exercise do, you might ask? In addition to contributing to your overall sense of wellness, exercise increases your production of endorphins, morphine-like neurotransmitters leading to a natural high.

Exercise can also improve your mood and self confidence as well as help you sleep better. Exercise such as running or swimming can put you into a kind of trance where your troubles become unimportant for the time being.

Speaking of trance, hypnosis and self-hypnosis are other options. You can learn to exist temporarily in another universe of your own creation. Breathing, meditation, tai chi and progressive muscle relaxation are other ways to find a calm space to inhabit for a while. Reading a good story sometimes provides the same benefit.

Finding a Balance

We have talked about people who lose themselves in work or other obligations. Others get lost in finding ways to escape their responsibilities. Neither pattern leads to overall satisfaction in the long run. Each creates its own form of stress.

The solution is to find a balance for your life in which you identify and pursue what is important to you with breaks to revive and refresh your body, mind and spirit. I don't know of any formula for finding the correct balance, but experimenting with the possibilities gives you a chance to get to know yourself, what you want, what you need and in what proportion.

Who Cares About You?

We talked before about people on your side. Most people, hopefully including you, have at least a few others in their life who really care about them. They might include family members who have known you from birth and friends you have from childhood or from school, jobs and sports.

Your relatives and friends care about you in different ways. Some might support you unconditionally no matter what. These are people you can always count on no matter what direction your life takes, for better or worse. You feel better just knowing they are there.

I cherish a few close friends like this. I can tell them anything about me, my dreams, my fears and my disappointments and mostly my joys. Sometimes they just listen, sometimes we work out plans together and sometimes they give me hints when I feel stuck in my life. I don't see them all on a regular basis, but I know they are there whenever I need them.

You might know some people in a certain context such as work. They may or may not know much about you in other circles besides the one you share during work hours. They are there for you when you clash with your boss, feel misunderstood or when you are ready to throw in the towel and look for another job.

How do such people help you prevent or minimize stress? Even if they can't keep you from facing stress, you know that you don't have to face it alone. These people will be there to encourage you, give you their support and advice and perhaps help you manage your stress if you need them to. I can't think of anything more stressful than trying to handle stress in a vacuum.

121

Call in the Reserves

In addition to your group of close supporters, other people can take the edge off acting alone. You can join or develop networks of like-minded people to face difficult tasks with you. They might not be front and center in your life all the time, but you can call on them in time of need.

If you need help, you can reach out to them before a crisis arises. If you know one is brewing, you can check with them for ideas on how to manage the coming crisis. Often they can help you handle minor issues while you face bigger challenges or possibly help you avert a crisis.

People Who Need People

In addition to your friends and relatives and reserve troops, how you interact with everyone else you meet along your life path can also prevent stress from arising or getting worse. Let's see how:

- You can connect with others for mutual support.

- You can become friends with others at church, social clubs or organizations or sports teams.

- You will meet people who continue as acquaintances you wave to or say hello to on a regular basis.

- Friendships can develop with these acquaintances.

- The more you share with others, the deeper your friendships will become.

- Some will become close friends and almost like family. These people take their place in the group of people who really care about you.

Recognizing and Owning Your Feelings

Some people don't pay much attention to their feelings. They might show signs of stress, possibly more obvious to others than to themselves, but they have trouble pinning these signs to their feelings.

Others are aware of how they feel but keep their emotions bottled up. That's like firing up a pressure cooker in your head. If untended, it eventually blows its top. If you have some or all the connections with people that we just discussed, share how you feel with them when the going gets tough.

Pleasant emotions are of course easier to share. Sharing them also enlivens people who care about you. What about negative emotions? If people you know bring out negative feelings in you, try talking with them about it. Blaming them for how you feel can make them defensive and perhaps angry with you. Besides, it does not solve anything.

There is a middle ground between keeping your feelings to yourself and blasting someone with them. You can say how you feel and also explain how your feelings are tied to what he or she is doing. Take responsibility for how you feel rather than blaming the other person.

You can also tell the other person that you feel the way you do whenever you are around them or when they do certain things which make you uncomfortable. Then you can have a conversation about how you feel rather than about what the other person did wrong.

Learn to be assertive, which is different from being aggressive. You don't want to attack others since they will start defending themselves and not hear what you have to say. You can be clear in presenting your goals, needs, interests or annoyances, owning each of them as yours.

Someone may take offense anyway, but then you can remind them that you are expressing what you think and feel and are not blaming them for how you feel. With practice, you can do this without attacking anyone else.

Knowing When to Say No

Learning to say no is another art. You can just say no and leave it at that or you can explain why you can't or won't do what someone may request from you. You have probably heard that "no" is a complete sentence.

Some people see themselves as full time caretakers in charge of everyone's needs. They feel a need to feel on duty all the time. For them, saying no is difficult. It takes practice to say no and mean it.

You are not obliged to explain yourself, but doing so might make it easier for the other person to understand and respect your decision. This does not always work. Some people just don't like being told no.

Then you have the choice of sticking to your guns or giving in to make them happy. It depends on what you can live with and how strongly you feel about setting limits on other people who would like to take advantage of you.

Stressful Topics of Conversation

You can probably think of topics about which you have very strong feelings. Most people do. Before engaging in a conversation, it might be best to know a little about the person with whom you are speaking. Does he or she fight tooth and nail to convince others of positions radically different from theirs? Unless you like all-out battles, you might want to be careful about venturing into certain topics with such a person.

You might encounter others who are more broad-minded, at least on less sensitive topics. Still, it would be better to introduce the topic as a question rather than implying that anyone who does not agree with you is a moron. If you do start gently and the other person jumps down your throat, a verbal war will not likely settle anything. Look for a graceful exit to a less volatile topic or find another person with whom to converse.

Toxic to Your Soul

We talked a little about toxic people earlier. If you know people to whom this heading applies, you are not alone. You can probably think of at least one person who drags you down into the mud with their venom at every opportunity. They start every conversation with "Did you hear about...?" and then launch an attack on every person they can think of.

My personal experience is that there is no way to navigate conversations with them. The best course seems to be to avoid them whenever possible and escape quickly if you get caught in their clutches. You don't stand much of a chance of changing their opinion. So why trouble yourself with more stress while expending wasted effort?

Making Assumptions about Relationships

In the past I made the assumption that all my friendships were mutual. I expected a positive response to my request when I asked for it from someone I had previously helped. My expectations were not always met.

If you are doing all the giving and get nothing back, you are a caretaker rather than a friend. If your request for help goes unnoticed or is resented, you might be wasting your time in a one way relationship.

Sometimes friends do not want your help. They prefer to solve problems at their own pace or in their own way without your input. They also may find your suggestions confusing or overwhelming. Sometimes people are not ready to change their lives and feel rushed by your efforts to help.

Friends struggling with alcoholism could feel that drinking is more comforting to them than it is damaging to their well-being. They might resent your attempts to help and see you as interfering in their lives. Trying harder to help might just increase the friction between you.

Insisting on being helpful when your input is not wanted might further damage your friendship. Your fruitless efforts might eventually draw you into your friends' difficulties without your being able to contribute anything. You might even end up spending more time and effort fretting about their problems than they do.

Sometimes your friends will tell you bluntly when your help is not wanted, saying their problems are none of your business. The message can also be more subtle. They might acknowledge your attempt to help but continue their self destructive behavior. Sometimes it is hard to tell when your efforts are appreciated or wanted.

It's not a bad idea to ask your friends if they would like your help with a particular problem. Or would they instead appreciate you listening to their struggles and being understanding of them? Maybe they would prefer to solve their own problems without your help. If they are honest with you, then you know whether to try helping or to back off.

If your efforts to help do not seem to be appreciated, you have several choices. You might tell your friends you would like to be helpful but realize they would prefer to tackle the problem on their own. You might check in with them from time to time to see how they are doing and ask them to let you know if you can be of help in the future. The most drastic step is to end your friendship if it seems more than you or the other person can bear comfortably.

It can be hard to accept that a friendship might be damaging to you but there are times when this might be the only reasonable conclusion. If a friend continues to choose a criminal lifestyle, to wallow in addiction rather than seeking help, or blames you for problems he or she has created, it might be time to step back from the friendship for a while or maybe even permanently.

Using Technology Judiciously

The Internet is touted as a wonderful tool bringing people together from the ends of the earth. You can interact with people you will likely never meet in person. We talked earlier about how technology can complicate your life as well as make it easier.

Studies of human communication indicate that most of what you convey is through channels other than your words. In addition to words, you communicate with tone of voice, gestures, body position, changes in skin tone, eye contact, pacing of your speech, pauses, touch, interpersonal space and odors such as pheromones, fragrances or even degree of cleanliness.

Hardly any of these enhancements can be found as part of electronic communication. Contact with others electronically seems to me to be becoming increasingly impersonal. The cryptic shorthand of text messages pares down your meaning to the bare bones and beyond.

More and more people seem to need almost minute by minute electronic contact with others. But in the process they offer and receive little by way of in-depth communication and, without realizing it, create opportunities for miscommunication and the stress it can cause. It would be wise to remain aware of these limitations to present day communication and realize how little of you actually gets sent with your text message. Sometimes the old fashioned way has its advantages.

Spiritual Stress Inoculation

With the Internet at your fingertips, you most likely have grown accustomed to expecting answers to your questions within seconds. Just ask Google. While this is often possible with factual questions, those questions involving the meaning of your life are not so easily answered, especially on the Internet. Not that there is any lack of opinions. It just seems that none of them are very satisfactory.

Thinkers in various religions have sought for centuries to explain the meaning of life and in the process have concocted many contradictory formulations and rituals to support them. Compounding the matter is that many religions think they have the one right way to understanding people, life and God. Obviously they can't all be right but maybe that's not the point.

Religions offer paths for you to take to connect with God and to make your way toward a way of life beyond the mundane. Holding a competition for the best religion does not seem to help anyone live a better life and has been the basis of more than a few wars throughout history.

Elizabeth Lesser in her book, *The New American Spirituality,* had this to say, "Religions are like cookbooks and guidebooks: they are not the food or the foreign country; rather, they suggest ingredients and point us in the right direction." Thich Nhat Hanh in a somewhat wider context wrote, "All systems of thought are guiding means: they are not the absolute truth."

Some people seek explicit guidelines for life and find them in their religion. They give very little independent thought to what they are taught and instead follow their faith, well, religiously. Others look to their religion for general guidance, interpreting church teachings as guidelines as Lesser and Hahn suggest. Non-religious people find guidance in humanist writings and in the example of people they admire.

With the backup of faith, believers face life tasks in accordance with the teachings of their church and feel a sense of assurance that they are on the right path. Many find the guarantee of salvation comforting as long as they follow the directives of their faith.

Religious rituals can provide comfort as well. When you grow up with them, rituals can remind you of familiar childhood times in later years. We talked earlier about how change is a significant part of stress.

Religious rituals can be a consistent part of your life reminding you that some things don't change. You can cling to them as familiar guideposts. At times when churches change their rituals, some of their adherents feel betrayed, while others feel that their church is keeping up with the times. It's hard to please everyone.

As we have seen, spirituality is a guide to life somewhat like that provided by religions. The goal is the same as for religion, but you are not asked to bind yourself to a specific set of beliefs or rituals. You are invited to see yourself in a larger context than that provided by your daily existence and to expand your understanding of your place in the universe.

For some, spirituality is not much different from religion and serves as a way to commune with God and the universe in a meaningful way. Yet the nature of spirituality seems hard to pin down. As we saw in Chapter 8, spirituality is a search to find a wider context for your life beyond the limited scope of your own daily existence.

So, what does spirituality mean in practice? For one thing it means letting go of control. Wait a minute. Isn't losing control one of the main contributors to stress? I don't think that's entirely true. It seems that the illusion of being out of control is what upsets you. Paradoxically, when you choose to let go of control, you are doing so voluntarily.

People often seek religion and spiritual practice for answers to questions they have about life. This search does not always yield satisfactory results. Perhaps a better mindset would be learning to live with your questions and sometimes seeing them as life's mysteries rather than always looking for easy answers.

So how do you do that? Slowing down is a big part of it. We have talked about the rat race which comprises life for many people. Slowing down requires stepping off the treadmill to regain your balance in life. You have a wide range of options for doing this. Let's look at a few of them.

The Breath of Life

Perhaps the easiest way and one often overlooked is to concentrate on your breath. Breathing is fundamental to your life. Try getting along without breathing for more than a few minutes. You most likely tend to take your breathing for granted unless you have had a serious respiratory illness or know someone who has suffered with one.

You can find a quiet space, close your eyes and pay attention to your breathing. Listen to it enter and leave your body. Most people tend to think of breath as flowing in and out of our lungs. To help you focus on it, try thinking of it as flowing out and then in rather than in and out. It seems like a small adjustment, but this kind of easy meditation can clear your mind and help you find a little peace.

Meditation

Most likely you have at least heard of meditation. Maybe you have even tried it. If you are not familiar with it, perhaps you see it is an exotic practice. When I entered the seminary, I had regular times for meditation in my schedule, but no one told me quite how to do it, at least to my satisfaction. I learned by trial and error that one way was to let my mind rest on the mysteries of the universe. There was no need to find answers to them as if they were riddles. Just sitting with these mysteries was enough to help me put aside my personal concerns, worries and obligations for a while.

Varieties of formal meditation practices abound. Yoga has become quite popular lately and has been practiced in eastern cultures for centuries. It consists of a series of poses usually including focus on breath and placing your body in various positions. New Age or other ethereal music often accompanies the practice.

Tai Chi is another discipline based on martial arts movements but not used for combat. A ritual series of slow focused forms, balance and deep breathing engage the body and mind.

These and other related practices date back many centuries and have been recognized by the Mayo Clinic among others as good ways to relieve stress. For our purpose at the moment you can consider meditation in all its forms as a spiritual practice to help you minimize the effects of stress on your mind and body as well as your spirit.

Henry David Thoreau and Oprah Winfrey

Do you know what these two luminaries have in common? Thoreau in his book, *Walden*, and Oprah in her daily talk show both followed and recommended taking time daily to write a list of what you are grateful for each day. Personally I find it a great way to keep my life in a positive context.

You are welcome to go about it any way you want. I start my list with "Thank you God for…" and then list at least five things for which I am grateful that day. Sometimes they are things I have anticipated for a long time. Sometimes they are complete surprises. Some are momentous but most are small delights which I would not savor if I did not take time to write them down. You might like to give it a try. Focusing on your sense of gratitude makes it harder to become overly upset by stress knocking at your door.

We have been looking at ways to avoid stress in this chapter. If you can't avoid it, you have two other choices. One is to confront it directly which we will consider in the next chapter. You can also transform stress into something useful and beneficial. We will consider this approach in Chapter 12.

Life Lab Lessons

- **How good are you at avoiding stress?** I don't know of anyone who can avoid it altogether. But maybe you have found some ways to keep stress at bay some or even most of the time. What are they?

- **List the ways you have learned to manage stress.** Post them somewhere where you can see them. As I mentioned before, you don't always think clearly under stress. It might be helpful to have your list handy when you most need it.

- **Have you tried organizing your life or even your day?** Did that make it easier for you to arrive at the end of the day in peace? If you haven't tried some of the ways to get organized which we mentioned in this chapter, why not give them a try to see if they help?

- **Part of being organized is to set priorities.** While you are trying out the use of lists, figure out which of the things on your list are most important and do them first.

- **You don't live in a vacuum.** Don't forget to talk about stress with people you care about you and compare notes with them. If things are really bad, there is also professional help to consider.

Chapter 11- Facing Stress Head-on

You can tell yourself that your stress is produced in your head and feel better. You still need to learn how to make a change.

~Alan Bernstein~

Toward the end of the last chapter, I noted that one way to avoid stress was to take it easy on yourself. You can choose to relax and accept life on its own terms rather than to try forcing it to be the way you want it to be. Some of the ways to approach stress either make it worse or just confuse you. Let's start with some approaches which do not work very well.

Accepting the Inevitable?

It is easy to see stress as a normal part of life. It's all around you and faces you at every turn. You will recall that people often choose to accept stress as a side effect of worthwhile goals. You also know now that stress can sneak up on you when you least expect it. But is stress inevitable?

Yes and no. Any time you are faced with change, stress lies waiting in the wings. It's unrealistic to think you can glide through life without the least bit of stress. But that doesn't mean you have to accept the inevitability of being crippled by stress or drowning in it. As you saw earlier, you have many ways to minimize stress. You will also see ways to turn it to your advantage.

Hiding from Stress

This sounds tempting at times. You could lock yourself away from the rest of the world and, if you can afford to, have everything delivered to your door. Howard Hughes tried it. Yet all indications are that his years of seclusion were not particularly peaceful or stress-free.

You might put distance between yourself and the causes of your stress. However, you would also need distance from your whole life. Living consists of growing physically, mentally, emotionally and spiritually and

131

accepting the associated stress of change which comes with growth. To avoid all stress, you would need to avoid all the life experiences which await you including the growth I just mentioned. Then you are stuck with no prospects for improving your life.

I Feel Fine

It's no fun to admit that you're dealing with stress. You can tell people you are doing well even when the bottom drops out of your world. You don't want anyone feeling sorry for you. Trying to handle stress alone is not a particularly effective way of going about it.

Why not? You don't have unlimited resources and knowledge. You don't know how to do everything. You are not Superman or Wonder Woman. Going it alone usually leads to a feeling of loneliness in addition to feeling overwhelmed, adding more stress to your already stressful situation. You make it worse by insisting that you can do everything on your own when you are unprepared to do so.

Accepting that you are a person with limitations only makes you a member of the human race. That's not so bad is it? You have company in your challenges. Everyone faces them. Most people who reach out to others for understanding and help find their challenges easier to face. Most likely, you will too.

You can try to convince yourself that you have no stress whatsoever. But denying it won't make it go away. You will spend more effort trying to bury your stress than it takes to face it head on and you will still be no closer to addressing the problem.

Who Can You Blame?

If you can't deny that you have stress in your life, what about blaming someone else for its presence? Quite a few possible culprits come to mind: God, your family, friends, coworkers, your boss, politicians and people in general. You can become so obsessed and exhausted looking for someone to blame for your stress that you have no energy left to do anything about it.

Making Others Suffer

Even if you don't find someone else to blame you might be tempted to take out your frustration on others. Perhaps you feel that your stress excuses you from acting like a normal human being. Being upset about your stress makes it okay to dump your feelings on others. Creating enemies is stressful too, so why add that to your woes? Flexing your quills like a porcupine makes others keep their distance and leaves you in that state of loneliness I mentioned above.

The Chemical Approach

Another way of trying to avoid stress is to hide in a chemical haze. Alcohol, mind altering drugs and street drugs can numb your mind and emotions, at least for a while. Prescription drugs can blunt your stress but not make it disappear. Drugs allow you to put aside your stress and block it out of your awareness for a while, but it doesn't go away permanently.

If you have tried this approach, you know that it is at best a temporary solution. Once you emerge from your fog, you find that nothing has changed, at least not for the better. If you do this on a regular basis, you will find your relationships, finances and indeed your whole life in tatters, creating much more stress than you started with. Plus the damage you do to your body in the process adds its own stress as well.

Put Off Until Tomorrow

Perhaps you remember Scarlett O'Hara's line from *Gone with the Wind*, "I'll think about that tomorrow." Maybe you have said this to yourself. And then tomorrow you say the same thing. After a while you have a pile of stressors waiting for your attention.

In addition to this pile is worry about others being upset with you for living in a dream world. You procrastinate, forget what you decided to ignore, and make your life even more complicated than it was before. To my mind, that's too much to worry about later!

133

Stress or Challenge?

Avoiding problems can work for a while. Yet, every new adventure arrives with its own problems. If the adventure is new to you, you don't have experience dealing with it and are likely to end up feeling stuck once in a while. Rather than facing new situations as problems, why not view them as challenges instead? That can help you feel a little more optimistic and more like a learner than a bungler. You just need to figure out how to best handle each new challenge as you proceed with your adventure.

Lost in Neverland

Earlier I mentioned hiding in technology such as cell phones and texting. You also have more passive ways of hiding in technology. Your television set will ramble on as long as you let it. I don't mean to say that TV can't be informative or entertaining. But if watching TV becomes a way of life, it can easily occupy most of your time. Although it distracts you from stress, it can also distract you from important things in your life.

In the long run, watching TV interminably only adds to your stress when you finally turn it off. You still have everything facing you that you did when you turned it on. It can be like coming down from a drug high. The pile of unfinished business has just grown higher while you were away from your life and lost in fantasy world.

The Internet is a little more interactive. You decide what sites to visit and what ads to watch or delete. The Internet can be a helpful tool if you use it as such and it is filled with useful information. Yet it can also serve as a magic carpet ride with little or no involvement of your mind or emotions. You can spend hours on the Internet and when you are done have no idea what you were doing.

Misery Loves Company

Before moving on to what does work in facing stress head-on, I would like to mention one last self-destructive approach. In the last chapter I talked about connecting with supportive people to help you stay focused and learning new ways to approach your stress.

Have you ever used others as a dumping ground for your problems? You don't really want their help but just want someone to hear your complaints. Even if they understand you and act in a supportive way, you aren't really listening to them.

If they offer suggestions, you ignore them and keep complaining. This process leads nowhere except further into the mire of self pity. Others will soon tire of hearing you whine while doing nothing about your situation. Remember what I said about loneliness? That's the next stop if you abuse or ignore your friends' attempts to help you.

Acknowledge the Problem

So what does work? Many of the approaches above are ways of denying your stress or trying to avoid thinking about it. If you want to find effective solutions, you must first acknowledge that there is a problem, or a challenge if you prefer.

I don't mean just stopping to notice that something is off kilter and then plodding along as if nothing happened. What I do mean is that you need to consider the problem in enough detail to understand it? Here are some questions to ask which may help:

- Where is my stress coming from?

- How does it make me feel?

- Have I experienced this before?

- How did I handle it?

- How well did my approach work?

With answers to these questions, you now know what you are facing and might well have some idea what to do about it.

How Does Stress Affect You?

Stress affects people in many different ways. Selye observed that it usually appears in the most vulnerable part of your body. How about vulnerable parts of your mind, emotions and soul as well?

You most likely have your own personal vulnerabilities. Your body is unique with its pattern of genes, its reaction to how you have treated it and its health depending on what you have fed it and what exercise you give it.

The rest of you including your mind, emotions and spirit are also unique. No one else has had quite the same set of experiences on any of these levels as those you have had. The sum total of all these experiences determines how stress will affect you for better or worse.

Strength you have gained through learning to handle past stress will help insulate you from falling apart under stress this time. Some people react very strongly to all their experiences, good or bad, as I mentioned earlier.

You may react with greater happiness and with deeper fear than others do. Or you may react to stress mostly on an intellectual level without paying much attention to how you feel about what is happening. You are too busy figuring out what to do about it.

The most effective approach to ongoing stress is taking time to understand your thoughts, feelings and reactions as well as their meaning for you as a person. This would also be a good time to take stock of your resources for meeting the current challenge. Success in dealing with past stress will help you feel confident in approaching new stressors. Frequent failure will make you more timid and fearful about facing new stressors.

Your ability to recall how you handled similar stressors in the past and knowing that you were able to manage them will help keep your stress in a manageable context. If you didn't find a satisfactory solution last time, asking someone for help with how to proceed might be a good idea.

Why Me?

You may wonder why you react to stress more or less strongly than others do. Research has indicated that family members growing up under the same conditions can react quite differently to just about any situation including stressful ones. Some seem never to recover from the traumas of their early life experiences and remain trapped in a hopeless existence. Others step out of the rubble, find a way to move beyond it and rebuild their lives.

While research as well as watching how people react to stress shows that they have constructive or destructive ways of reacting to stress, I have not seen any adequate explanation for why people differ so much in their reaction to stress. Why do some people crumble and others rise from the ashes? Psychologists invented a handy term known as "individual differences."

The bottom line is that you have your own unique set of experiences and reactions to everything which happens in your life. Your body, mind, emotions and soul come together to determine how you deal with life and all its complexities, including stress. I know this is not very specific but it takes into account that no two people are quite the same. You shouldn't be surprised if you handle things very differently from people around you, including your own family members.

Own Your Stress

This chapter began by looking at many of the ways to deny or avoid dealing with stress. To find an effective approach, you must own your stress. Yes, it is yours, making your life difficult and blocking you from where you want to be in life. Of course, I am speaking here of chronic stress.

At the beginning of this book, I told you that acute stress is a warning sign of imminent danger which can be quite useful in keeping you safe from harm. Owning your stress means not blaming others for it, not trying to make it someone else's problem, not denying that you have any stress and not ignoring it.

Your Turn to Shine

Your stress is yours and it's up to you to decide what to do about it. No one else can do it for you. Where is your fairy godmother when you need her? The reality is that she doesn't exist. You're on your own. Well, not quite. You heard earlier that you probably have a group of people who can offer support and suggestions, making the burden a little easier for you.

Even with support, encouragement and suggestions, you are still the one who must choose among the various possibilities for how to proceed. It is up to you to weigh suggestions from your supporters and decide how useful they are for you. Seldom is there only one approach to dealing with any kind of stress.

During the course of our journey together, we have seen quite a variety of causes for stress as well as the many levels on which stress affects you.

You need to find an individualized approach to handling your stress and you are the only individual who can do so.

Where to Start

With serious stress, plenty is happening on all levels. Your body shuts down non-essential functions, your mind moves into high gear, your emotions roil, and your soul might be rocked to its foundation. So much is happening at once that it can seem like a hopeless jumble.

If you have ever tried to do too many things at once, you will realize that you end up doing none of them well. To make it easier, or maybe even just possible, try looking at the various aspects of your stress one at a time. Now that you know what doesn't work very well, here are some helpful steps.

Banishing Unhelpful Beliefs

I have not yet mentioned unhelpful beliefs. Here are a few of them:

- I am dealing with stress which is beyond my capability.

- I might just as well give up. There is nothing I can do.

- Nobody could deal with the stress I am facing right now.

These are some unproductive thoughts you might have. But what do you do about them? Here are some ways to get started:

- Listen to the thoughts passing through your mind, both the helpful and unhelpful ones. Write them down and see if they make any sense to you.

- Mark the thoughts that are not true or even ridiculous.

- Cross them off and stop thinking about them.

- Concentrate on the thoughts that offer possibilities for dealing with your stress.

Divide and Conquer

In earlier chapters, you saw how stress affects your body, mind, emotions and spirit. Now consider how your stress affects you in a personal way. I talked before about how lists can help you get organized in your approach to understanding and dealing with stress. Begin by making separate lists of how your stress affects you on each of the levels I mentioned.

You might react quite differently from the way others would in your situation. Your response is unique. Talking to others or reading about their stress might give you some ideas but will probably not address your unique situation. There is no easy formula. This is your journey although others may have trodden similar paths.

Your Mindset

Trying to make sense of your stress does not work very well while you are in panic mode. You can't think clearly. The best way to approach stress is calmly and rationally. Then you can take the time you need to carefully document your stress and its effects on you. If your emotions are astir right now, this might not be a good time for you to try making sense of your stress. But you don't want to stay stuck either. I will talk more about stress in a moment, but first let's focus on getting your mind to focus.

Take your Time

Your first impulse might be to try getting your stress behind you as quickly as possible. If you are like most people, that certainly is the way you have learned to approach almost everything unpleasant in your life.

Rushing through tasks is no more effective that trying to do everything at once. If you haven't learned to be patient with yourself, this would be a good time to start developing the skill for when it will be needed. Here are some ways to do it:

- Begin with the breathing and meditation exercises I mentioned in the last chapter.

- Slow down you mind by focusing on just being still and allow your body to relax as a starting point.

139

- Practice getting out of the panic mode and into a more constructive frame of mind.

- Next proceed to facing the problem more calmly and rationally.

- If you need to develop this skill, I would suggest working on it before you need it in an emergency situation.

Avoiding Distractions

Learning to deal with stress is hard work. It takes concentration and single-mindedness. Friends will try being helpful by distracting you from your stress and encouraging you to get your mind on something else. There is nothing wrong with this as long as it remains a refreshing break before you get back to the business at hand.

You may be tempted to take a permanent break from the struggle. But staying on break indefinitely does not solve your problem. It certainly would be easier than the hard work you are doing to solve your problem. Yet your job will not finish itself. Sooner or later life will remind you that you have unfinished business needing your attention. It would be better to stick with it and finish it now rather than letting it linger on and burden you indefinitely.

Stick with Your Agenda

It feels good to finally get your life back on course. You might even be tempted to try to rearrange your whole life rather than just addressing the current stressors. That's a noble aspiration but makes it hard to focus on the details and keep them straight. Trying to do everything at once will most likely leave you feeling that you aren't doing a good job with anything.

I mentioned making lists to help organize your thinking about stress and how you tackle it. Know what you want to accomplish and set up an agenda for approaching it methodically. It will then be easier to stay on task and deal with the issues important to your quest.

Feelings

Try listing all your feelings about your present stress and how those feelings affect you. Once you have an understanding of the emotions involved and have found a way to deal with them, you should be able to proceed more calmly and rationally, keeping your emotions under control as you do so.

Does that sound a little too simple? Do you approach your feelings and emotions calmly and rationally? You can use your lists to chart the feelings which accompany your stress. As you deal with stress, you can consider what feelings arise, what triggers them and how they affect you.

Okay, how about an example? Suppose you are in a relationship which you thought was going well and suddenly you find yourself jilted and alone again. What emotions does this predicament trigger in you? Here are some typical reactions:

- Abandonment.

- Loneliness.

- Anger.

- Sadness.

- Grief.

- Guilt.

I have touched on most of these emotional reactions along the way. Let's look at the first two in a little more detail. Obviously the breakup is a major contributor to your feeling of being abandoned. Maybe there are other contributors as well.

Perhaps one of your parents left your family when you were a young child. Your sense of abandonment in your current relationship might well trigger recall of similar feelings in childhood. Bringing them back to your awareness distracts you from your efforts to resolve the current problem. It feels like someone pushed you back into a pit from which you thought you had successfully emerged.

Let's look at loneliness, and how it affects you. Your relationship gave you a sense of context and belonging. You thought you were important to someone who cared about you, not to mention that you had someone to care about. Now, when something good happens you do not have anyone to share it with. The same is also true when something bad happens.

Keeping Stress in Perspective

When something stressful arises, sometimes you will be tempted to consider it a catastrophe, the worst thing that could possibly happen. With some reflection, you realize that it is not the end of the world. Perhaps you have faced the same or worse stress in the past or know others who have survived what you now face. You can also recall what worked for you in the past.

If this is your first time facing major stress, think of others you know who have faced stress similar to yours. Maybe they can help you with your challenge. For more on feeling in the depths of a catastrophe and overreacting to stress, see Albert Ellis and Robert Harper's book, *A New Guide to Rational Living*.

Even if you feel devastated, you are still alive. Be grateful for those who offer help to keep you going until you get back on your feet again. In the section on the dark night of the soul, I mentioned that there are ways to transform stress into something meaningful for your life. You will hear more about this in the next chapter.

Your Coping Strategies

So far, you have seen ineffective ways to approach stress when it finds you. You have also seen some better ways to approach it. Now let's get more specific and see what tools you can use in approaching your stress. I will present a few of the more common ones.

With practice, you will learn to refine these and develop new ones which work well for you and to set aside those which are not as useful. You might have skills you don't know you have or maybe ones you have forgotten about. Perhaps this discussion will bring back to mind some of your rusty resources.

Gratitude

In the last chapter, I talked about a gratitude list and an attitude of gratitude as good ways to help cushion you from the impact of stress and as ways to lessen its effect when it arrives in your life. Staying mindful of all the blessings in your life helps you keep your stressors in context and prevents you from falling into despair in which you see your life as hopeless.

An attitude of gratitude helps you keep your perspective in times of stress. When you feel overwhelmed, you can take a little time to ponder the riches in your life. It might be a little harder to focus on them while you are struggling with stress. If you have kept a gratitude journal on a regular basis, this might be a good time to open it and look back to see the blessings you received each day in the past.

Can You Change Your Situation?

Reinhold Niebuhr prayed as follows, "God grant me the serenity to accept the things I cannot change, the courage to change the things I can change, and the wisdom to know the difference." This prayer has been adopted by many AA members. Not everyone in AA believes in God, although there is a general consensus that there exists a higher power beyond their comprehension to which everyone can turn for comfort and guidance.

Maybe this would be a good tool to use first. You have seen that it is harder to deal with things on your own than it is with help. If God cannot help you, who can? I also talked about seeing your stress in context. What greater context is there than being a creature in God's universe?

When you say this prayer, you are asking God to help you be realistic. It is not always easy to know what is possible and what is not. After praying and reviewing your resources, you should have a better idea about whether your plan to deal with stress is realistic. Suppose you conclude that the stress you face is impossible to change. Maybe someone very close to you has died. Bringing that person back to life is not an option.

Saying it is not fair, too soon or can't be happening doesn't change the facts either. Not being able to change what has happened does not mean you are out of options. You can't undo what has happened but you can make some changes in your life to compensate for what you have lost. This is best done through the process of transformation which I will talk about in the next chapter.

As I have said several times, Selye described stress as the response to a demand for change. Change is always stressful, whether you have chosen it or not. Change requires courage since you are stepping into the unknown and have no guarantee of where your path will take you.

143

A theologian I once knew, Father Augustine Hennessey, described marriage as jumping off a cliff and asking God to find you a soft landing. Many other life ventures are equally uncharted. If you decide that a particular stressor is one you can tackle, with or without help, it's time to bring out your private arsenal.

Eyes on the Goal

To accomplish this task, it would be helpful to keep a journal of your efforts in dealing with troublesome situations. Once you know your goal, keep track of what steps you try, what works and what doesn't.

If this is the first time you have faced this particular stressor, you might benefit from consultation or guidance from people you trust. Another approach is to use the trial and error method. You might be successful on your own, but it is usually faster and simpler with some help.

As you start dealing with your stress, remember what you want to accomplish. Once you understand where your stress comes from and how it affects you, your main goal is to deal with the stressors which face you. Maybe you can make them disappear or maybe you can lessen their effect on you.

If none of this is possible, perhaps you can transform your stress into something useful in your life as you will soon see. That's the long term goal. Once you find a goal which seems realistic, note it for the next time in case this stressor resurfaces.

Now it's time to ask yourself some more questions:

- How will I get to where I want to be?
- Can I handle this on my own?
- Who can help me if I get stuck?

Perhaps you will be able to proceed smoothly. But prepare yourself for setbacks. You may not succeed immediately in your first attempt to solve the problem. If not, you will need to change your goals or your plan to reach them and find an approach which works better for you.

Get Organized with Your Stress

Once you know what your stressors are and how they affect you it's time to take action. But what action should do you take first? If you have some ideas write them down. Remember this is likely to be a confusing time and you might forget where you are in your plan.

The order in which you list the steps of your plan doesn't matter right now. This is brainstorming time. It is also a good time to get suggestions from those who care about you and from those you know have undergone the same or similar trials.

With this information in hand, you can look over your list and decide which step to take first. You don't have to do this by yourself if someone is helping you with your quest. But remember that this is your stress.

Your plan might well differ from someone else's. How you proceed will depend on how well you have done responding to stress in the past, especially to stressors like the one you are facing now. Also important are how much confidence you have in yourself and what attitude you take toward your stress.

Another thing to remember is flexibility. If you have not faced this particular stressor before, you will not know exactly how to handle it. You may have some ideas of your own or have gotten help from others who have faced similar situations.

If you can't think of anything which worked for you with a similar stressor in the past, you might need to try additional approaches at your disposal to see how well they work. If you don't achieve the results you want, don't just give up. It's time to tweak your approach until you find one that works better for you.

You Are Not In It Alone

So far I have been talking mostly about stress which involves just you. That's not quite true though. People who care about you will be affected by your stress because what happens to you is important to them.

Sometimes stress results from a problem between you and someone else. It's hard enough to keep straight what's going on in your own mind in times of stress. You have your own priorities, ways of looking at the problem and your own agenda. But now there is someone else to take into account. Here are some things to consider when someone else shares your stress, especially when you are in conflict:

- **Resolving the conflict should be your main goal.** Winning an argument is not likely to reduce stress. The other person involved might feel defeated and continue aggravating you after you think it's all over. Finding a mutually agreeable resolution is your best bet for a peaceful aftermath.

- **Focus on the here and now.** Warring couples are famous for kitchen sink arguments. They drag in everything that has bothered them over the past twenty years. This just adds to the resentment and makes it more difficult to focus on the task at hand. If you have other issues to resolve, wait until another time.

- **Pick your battles.** This is similar to the approach in the last point. Agree to settle one issue at a time. Learn to set aside minor issues which aggravate you but are not of critical importance or part of the current problem.

- **Attend to what the other person says and feels.** In the heat of conflict, people want to get their point across without bothering to understand the other side. Maybe you can shout down the other person, but that doesn't resolve anything, although you might feel better at the moment. You can ask for clarification of what is meant at any point. Also, you can ask the other person to share what he or she feels about the matter and wants to accomplish.

- **Be willing to forgive.** In a two person conflict, it usually turns out that both parties have contributed to the hostilities. Admit to and apologize for your part in the conflict and be willing to forgive the other person especially when he or she apologizes.

- **Know when to let go of something.** Not everything that comes up in discussion of your conflict is important. Stick to the main issues and don't let side issues distract you.

- **Tell the other person how much you appreciate their efforts.** Both of you are working on the problem, hopefully together. Appreciating the other person's efforts makes it easier for both of you to stay focused and work together.

Caring for Your Body

Most of what you have seen so far in this chapter has to do with what's going on in your mind. I spoke earlier in the book about the effects of stress on the body. Lets look a little at what you can do for your body when it is under stress.

- **Get some rest.** Stress takes a toll on the body as you have seen. It can easily wear you down. Rest is essential. Without it, your body will tire of its attempts to cope with stress. Your mind becomes dull as well. Preparing for sleep is easy to take for granted. Television does not set the mood for restful sleep. It would be better to turn it off well before bedtime.

- **Save it for later.** Just before bed is not the ideal time to wrestle with your stress either. If something important related to your stress occurs to you just before sleep, write it down and think about it tomorrow. Choose relaxing activities such as reading or listening to soothing music instead of television to prepare for sleep.

- **Eat well.** Appetite often changes with stress as well. Maybe you feel a need to comfort yourself with food that tastes good but provides little nutrition. You don't do yourself any favors with careless eating in times of stress. At the other extreme, you might lose interest in food when you are overwhelmed by stress. It is hard to depend on your appetite to tell you when you need food in these circumstances. Maintaining proper nutrition needs to be a conscious choice during stressful periods. You can also add this to your written plan.

- **Exercise is also important.** Adrenalin tenses the body when it is under stress. Exercise is a good way to release this tension. It also helps with digestion and rest.

- **Learn to relax your muscles.** Related to exercise but also akin to meditation is muscle relaxation. In 1938, the psychologist Carl Jacobson developed a series of exercises known as progressive muscle relaxation. You can find descriptions and recordings of how to do it on places like Amazon. YouTube is another possibility.

    If you want to try it on your own, here's how. Lie in a comfortable place on your back wearing loose clothing. You can take a few deep breaths to get you in the relaxing mood. Then tense the muscles throughout your body starting with your feet. Hold the

147

tension in each muscle group for a few seconds and then release your muscles. Then notice the difference. Work your way up your body isolating all the various muscle groups from your feet up to your scalp.

- **Honor your breath.** I mentioned breathing earlier. Breathing out and in slowly and concentrating only on your breath while clearing your mind of everything else combines physical and spiritual approaches. It is a very simple form of meditation, but quite effective.

  You usually think of breathing in and then breathing out. To stay more focused, think of breathing out and then breathing in to help you concentrate on what you are doing. Breathing and muscle relaxation also serve as good preparations for sleep just before bedtime.

Spiritual Coping

I just mentioned meditation and breathing. Your breathing is critical to life. Try staying alive without it. Spirituality is about treasuring your life and living in a larger context than your own interests. Respecting your breath is a good way to begin seeing yourself in a larger context. Remember that the oxygen you breathe has circulated through all living creatures as long as they have inhabited the earth. That should also give you some sense of a larger context.

Meditation is an extension of your focus on breathing. Our culture encourages scurrying around at a frenetic pace. Meditation takes place at the opposite pole. It involves slowing down of the body and mind for a period of reflection.

Eastern spiritual traditions employ meditation with a focus on nothingness, emptying your mind and ignoring your ego, or sense of self, to merge with the world and universe. Western spiritual traditions see meditation as a way of filtering out distractions and living fully in the present moment in search of an inner calm and peace. In the Christian tradition, meditation involves contemplating the mysteries of faith rather than being absorbed by daily events and concerns.

Elizabeth Lesser, whom I mentioned earlier, presents one of the chief benefits of meditation in times of stress. She states, "Meditation helps us separate the fact of stress from our anxious reactions to it." Stress may be present in your life at the moment. But that doesn't mean you need to spend all your time obsessing over it and in the process adding more stress.

Through meditation, you can come to understand that, despite your current stress, you are still who you are with all the good things in your life despite the onslaught of stress. I will talk more about spirituality in the next chapter when our journey takes us to the topic of transforming or reframing stress.

When You Get Stuck

You are more likely to get stuck when dealing with unfamiliar stress. You will have to use a trial and error approach more often while covering new ground. Sometimes what you try will not work, at least not as well as you would like it to. The key is not to get discouraged and give up too easily. There are plenty more approaches to try. But at some point you might run out of ideas and still have not found a solution.

Then it's time to go back to the drawing board. You may be aware of books besides this one, articles or videos on stress you can consult. If not, your library or Google can help you discover quite a variety of resources. You can ask your friends or family what they would recommend. They might know of something you have not tried or even considered.

Another option would be to consult a mental health professional. Counselors, psychologists and social workers deal with it all the time. Clergy are usually quite familiar with stress as well.

Life Lab Lessons

- **Trust Yourself.** By now you should know quite a bit about stress: what it is, where it comes from, how to minimize it and how to face it. Don't be afraid to use what you have learned in your battle with stress.

- **Use all your resources.** Some people think they need to find the one best tool and use that exclusively. You have seen how stress affects you on many different levels. You might need to deal with your stress on several different fronts at the same time.

149

- **Track what works in your adventure with stress.** Write down where you want to be, what you need to do to get there, what you have tried and what works for you as you go along in the journey toward stress resolution.

- **Don't stay stuck.** Some of what you try might not work as well as you hope. Especially with a new kind of stress, you might have to try several approaches before you find one that works for you.

- **Don't leave your posse back at the ranch.** Your supporters might give you some ideas where to start dealing with your stress. They can be just as helpful deciding what works for you once you get started. They might see progress you have trouble seeing for yourself.

- **Stay flexible.** Don't be afraid to let go of approaches which don't work as well as you expected. You can tweak them or discard them, trading them in for better approaches. Once you get started, it might also be easier to see new possibilities.

Chapter 12- Transforming Stress

The greatest weapon against stress
is our ability to choose one thought over another.

~William James~

So far in our journey together, we have discovered what stress is, where it comes from, some of the ways it affects you, how to prevent or minimize it, what to do if it finds you anyway and ways it can be useful. We haven't yet considered how you can use it to improve your life. Did you know that was possible?

In Chapter 8 we discussed the relationship between stress and spirituality. We saw how stress can affect your spirituality and how spirituality can help you cope with stress. Now we will see how approaching stress in a spiritual way can help you enrich your life through your experience of stress.

This is likely a bit foreign to your usual way of thinking about stress and maybe about spirituality as well. You might be tempted to just ignore your stress and move on with your life. Even if you could do so, you would miss a valuable opportunity to improve your life.

Returning to the Dark Night of the Soul

The dark night of the soul represents an extreme experience of almost overwhelming stress. Without spiritual resources, some people become overwhelmed and despair even to the point of considering or attempting suicide. Let's look a little more closely at the dark night we discussed in Chapter 8.

If you have not read Thomas Moore's book, *Dark Night of the Soul: a Guide to Finding Your Way Through Life's Ordeals*, you might want to do so or at least put it on your list for later reading. You can see Moore's more detailed account of the topics considered here.

In our previous discussion, you learned about how very taxing experiences take you away from your ordinary routine. They challenge everything you thought you knew about yourself and your life. You may have thought you knew where you were headed in life, but such experiences offer you the

151

opportunity to re-examine your beliefs, assumptions and goals. What you thought you knew about yourself might not make much sense now as the dark night descends.

Recall our talking about out the nature of stress as leaving you with a feeling of being out of control. I have spent most of this book showing you how to understand and deal with stress by regaining control of your life. Yet John of the Cross and Thomas Moore encourage you to surrender control and give in to the state of unknowing at least for a while as you attend to the mystery of your existence.

Heavy stuff! This may seem like letting stress win. I don't think it is. To my mind, it means letting go of control for the time being while you look beyond your present circumstances, dire though they may be, to reach a deeper understanding of yourself, your resources and your place in the universe.

Dark nights, like all forms of stress, create trials for you. You have two ways of thinking about them. You can see them as roadblocks to overcome or chances to understand yourself better. The second approach takes more time and energy but gives you an opportunity to use it to better advantage and prepare yourself for future stress.

The route you choose depends on whether knowing yourself better and improving your life skills is important to you. No matter which you choose, your stress is likely to be around for a while until it resolves itself or you find a way to manage it. In the meantime, you can stew over your unpleasant circumstances or you can put this experience to good use.

Beyond the Obvious

Whether you are dealing with a dark night or a lesser form of stress, the experience is unsettling and disturbs your ordinary routine. If it is a new stress for you, it might take you by surprise and present you with circumstances beyond your understanding and current ability to manage it.

In that sense, it's not just a problem but a learning opportunity. Did you know that insanity can be a bad habit? I mentioned earlier that insanity can be defined as doing the same thing over and over and expecting a different result.

You have seen that destructive attempts to cope with stress include dealing with it through alcohol or other drugs. You feel better for a little while, but the problem doesn't go away. Usually it becomes compounded by your struggle with chemicals.

Stress often calls on you to rely on something beyond your personal capacity or at least beyond what you think is your capacity. You do not know how much you can stand. Sometimes you think you are approaching your limit and indeed you might be at that limit. We have already talked about getting help when you need it. Seeking help may be the best route for you to take at this moment in time.

Back to Basics or Beyond Them

Medical and psychological interventions are geared to returning you to your level of functioning before you encountered a particular stressor. Selye thought people had an optimal level of functioning. More recent research suggests that you do not have one best level of functioning but rather a range of functioning which varies from one situation to another.

As you might recall, Ruiz talked about this in his book, *The Four Agreements*. The fourth agreement is to always do your best. He pointed out that your best can vary considerably from one moment to another. In times of great stress, it would be reasonable to expect that your best would be diminished by stressful circumstances at least for a while.

Be kind to yourself and don't expect too much under duress. Concentrate on taking care of yourself rather than trying to push yourself back to "normal." Once you recover, you will find your old skills returning. Have patience. In facing this trial, you will gain some new skills and a better understanding of yourself in the process.

Alternate Ways to Express Yourself

Moore also talked about trying new ways to communicate if your normal channels are blocked, which they might well be under severe stress. People often try to explain away their stress or make excuses for being stuck.

He suggests that you try ways of communicating and expressing yourself other than your normal language. These ways might include storytelling, symbolism, metaphor, art and music. It's at least worth a try. Normal conversation might be inadequate for expressing how you think and feel under great stress. You might not have words for what is happening to you.

153

Taking an alternate approach does not work the same way for everyone. I once knew two artists who had periodic trouble with serious depression. One found that he could only paint when he was in a state of depression. He had learned to transform the stress of his depression into artistic expression. The other artist could only produce his art when depression left him. During periods of depression he had to find other outlets and resources. Spending time on the lake in his sailboat helped him as did counseling and medication.

If your stress does not lead you to life threatening depths in which you need medical intervention, you can use the experience to spend some time with yourself, learning to understand the range of your emotions as well as your ability to survive and perhaps thrive under stress. Prayer at this time can often help while you wrestle with the experience of your pain.

Life Mysteries

Many religions will tell you that your stressful times are part of God's will and plan for you. Some people who accept this explanation find a way to adapt their lives to live under circumstances which might not make sense to them. Others find the idea of God's willing bad experiences for them or for those they love very hard to accept.

They wonder why a loving God would impose such a trial on them. They might think that they have brought difficulties on themselves. If they had lived a better life, God would not be punishing them now. Some blame God for getting them into this mess and some stop believing in God altogether as a result.

The Mysteries of Everyday Life

It seems these days that people want to understand, explain and find a use for everything they encounter. If you get stuck, you can find an answer on Google. You will be tempted to become so involved in the practical that you completely miss most of the little delights along your life path. This seems especially true of things which have no easy explanation.

At the end of the day, many people add up what they have accomplished that day since they got out of bed. I wonder how many people count the little delights which have passed their way during the day. Remember the gratitude list? If you become too busy with the practical, you will most likely miss the fanciful which can be a refreshing change.

What is the meaning of your life? If you just count what you accomplish in a day, you have a list and start a new one the next day. But there is more to life than keeping score if you allow the unknown into your awareness. I am talking about the little mysteries which present themselves along your path.

Here are a few which might catch your attention at least for a moment:

- How do two incomplete cells become a human being or any other life form?

- How does our solar system stay in balance century after century?

- How does a single atom stay in balance for that matter?

- How does you mind interpret what your senses encounter?

- What does it mean to fall in love with someone?

You could most likely find scientific explanations for all these mysteries and consider the problem solved. What if you don't seek practical answers right away or even at all? What if you ponder these mysteries and coexist with them for a while? You move to a different plane of existence beyond the practical. Art and music also have meaning for you beyond what you can express in words.

The same can be true of life mysteries you encounter. A newspaper critic can tell you how well music was performed technically. But a critic can't tell you whether or how music touches your soul. The same is true of any other form of art. Your experience is beyond the technical aspects and is unique to you. Philosophers are in agreement that you can't argue about taste.

No one else's sense of appreciation is quite like yours. Did you ever try to explain your artistic taste to someone else? Not so easy, is it? The same can be said of your experience of nature, the world, other people and especially the unique aspects of yourself as a person. It is a different way to exist but you might want to try it at least for a while.

You might also consider stress as somewhat of a mystery. We have seen where stress comes from and what it does to you. We have also looked at what you can do about it. The one remaining question is why this is happening to you. We have seen that some stress is self imposed, sometimes in exchange for definite benefits. But there still might be no adequate explanation for why you find yourself stressed out right now.

Rather than torturing yourself for answers which don't exist, you might try adding your unsolved questions to the list of life's mysteries, a few of which I listed above. That way you can put what happened to you into a basket with other unexplained events in your life and get on with the process of living rather than torturing yourself to find answers for elusive questions.

Here is how Moore sums it up, "A dark night of the soul is dark because it doesn't give us an assurance that what is happening makes sense and will be beneficial." You can spend your time chasing answers and explanations indefinitely. As an alternative you can accept the mystery of your trials and instead concentrate on what you can learn from them as well as how you can use that knowledge in the future.

Perhaps you have lived by rigid rules for conducting your life, handed down by your family or church. Maybe at least some of what you learned can be of help with extreme stress. You now have a chance to learn some new ways of coping which will help you be more flexible in approaching and managing future stress. Your new-found flexibility results from your efforts to transform your stress.

Life Lab Lessons

- **Don't be afraid of the dark night.** It is not your decision to go there. It is one of the stress states which settle down upon you. You don't have a choice of whether to be there. You do have a choice of how to approach it and what you learn from it.

- **Accept as your best whatever you are able to do under stress.** Don't be too hard on yourself or expect too much when you are heavily burdened.

- **Accept the mysteries of life as they unfold around you.** Don't try to make logical sense of everything that happens. Sometimes you can just watch the world go by and view it with interest.

- **Try different ways to express yourself.** Experiment with painting, whether or not you produce a masterpiece. Clay sculpture feels good in your hands no matter what emerges. You can sing to yourself to your heart's content.

- **Be patient with the unknown.** You don't know where your life is headed. No matter how bad things seem now, you will most likely find better times in the future.

Chapter 13- The Future of Stress

The illiterate of the future will not be
those who cannot read and write,
but those who cannot learn, unlearn and relearn.

~Alvin Toffler~

Where do we go from here? No one I know has the ability to predict the future accurately. So I won't pretend I can either. At the beginning of this book, we considered variations of stress from one set of circumstances to another. We also looked at stress you assume for good or bad reasons and stress which finds you regardless of how you live your life.

What's next for your life? You can imagine what might happen, based on how your life has gone up to now. There are only three possibilities. Things can stay the same. They can get worse. They can get better.

Stress in your life and how you respond to it will not magically change. Your life will only be different if you learn different ways to live in various circumstances. I have noted that stress is part of your everyday life, a built-in part of you which helps you respond to immediate danger. But stress is also a part of daily living and a side effect of many of the life decisions you make.

I have also shared with you various ways to prevent and minimize stress, face it head-on and transform it into something meaningful and helpful for your life. You have learned how to understand stress and also what you can do about it. But, as we have also seen, there is more to life than what takes place inside you.

Part of your stress comes from the environment in which you live. But your environment might change. How your environment changes in the future will affect your level of stress. How society changes will also affect your stress level.

You will learn here how societal changes might affect your stress level. None of the approaches we discuss here will be of any lasting effect if you do your part only occasionally or not at all. You will need to develop some new habits which we will also consider.

157

A Healthy Environment

Earlier we saw how your health affects your stress level and how your stress level affects your health. Now let's look at how your environment contributes to your health and how the earth's future will affect your future stress.

At the broadest level, we all share the earth's environment. Scientists are in almost universal agreement that the earth is experiencing a period of global warming. Yet people continue to disagree about the extent to which this development is due to the way we treat our environment.

The earth has experienced long periods of warming and cooling over the ages. Yet now the earth's people are busy dumping millions of tons of industrial and personal lifestyle pollutants into the sky. Despite some efforts to curb this pattern of poisoning the earth's environment, so far there is no global commitment to do so.

Short term profit remains a higher priority than a healthy earth. Air and water quality continue to suffer even though both are critical to human survival as well as to the survival of other animals and plants, indeed the health of all living things. We have already considered the stress associated with illness. We as a global people can make a difference in our health if we make it our priority and consequently reduce our global stress level with better choices in caring for our environment.

Food Sources

At one time most people planted or raised at least some of their own food. Much of the food our recent ancestors ate came from farms not too far away from where they lived. Now our foods come mostly from industrial and farm factories and are often shipped from the far flung corners of the earth. As food has become a big business, chemical fertilizers, preservatives, genetic modification of food and growth hormones have appeared on the scene to maximize production and profit.

Now much of our food comes packaged and treated with a variety of chemicals to extend shelf life and appeal to our taste buds. If your body had a vote, it would most likely veto much of what most people put on their plate. For most of the last few decades, we have had little understanding of what is in our food or what passes as food.

More recently, packaging laws at least gave us the opportunity to find out what the packages really contain. Our food frequently arrives cooked, sugared and salted in wrappers and bags at drive-through windows. We gobble what we buy as we rush on to the next event in our busy lives. We don't even have a chance to savor what we eat.

Yet farm markets and stands have started appearing with more regularity in many parts of the country and have always been available locally in less developed countries. We are starting to know our food producers again, buying fresh fruits and vegetables and relearning how to prepare our own recipes rather than living out of cans, packages and boxes.

If the trend toward food awareness and care in what we eat continues, it will reduce stress because of the overall health benefits. Gardening in itself reduces stress, whether or not you produce anything edible. If you haven't experienced the joy of eating a fresh tomato you grew from a seedling, you should try it.

The Global Community

We give lip service to considering ourselves a world family. Yet we seldom view people in other countries as part of "us." We tend to understand little about how most other people live and often feel no personal connection with them unless we have traveled to their country Even then, we are likely to visit only the tourist spots.

Yet everyone is subject to the environmental and nutritional concerns I just mentioned. We are all in this together whether we like it or not and whether or not we are willing to admit it or do anything about our nutrition. It is easy to look after our own interests and leave others to their own devices. Many cultures including our own have viewed others as somewhat less than human or at least inferior to their own natives.

Our misunderstanding and indifference toward other cultures is in my opinion the basis of the many wars we have endured through the ages. If we could make understanding each other a priority, war would be much less likely. So would the severe stress it causes participants on both sides of the struggle no matter who ends up winning any particular conflict.

Local Environment

Our environment is not just a global one. Most of us live in villages, towns or cities. We find ourselves packed together to the point where our lifestyles rub up against each other. Meeting your neighbors will quickly teach you that others have ways of living far different from yours. Their music might jar your nerves. Their barking dog does little to delight you. The way they keep their yard might not be to your liking. Overlap of family environments becomes exaggerated with apartment living. It often involves living close to people you would prefer to have living a little farther away from you.

You don't have a choice of who lives next to you unless you own the whole block or apartment house. You can move if you don't like your neighbors but moving is one of the chief sources of stress. Even if you do move, you don't know if your new neighbors will suit you any better.

Attachment to electronics makes it more difficult to interact with other actual people around you. Being plugged into various devices tends to make you oblivious to others although it might make you feel more connected. Isolation encourages you to think of yourself as an individual rather than as a citizen of a common community.

At one time, families shared a common environment. Farm families worked together for their mutual subsistence and survival. Before the advent of personal electronics, family members might have gone their own ways during the day but ate together at home in the evening. They spent their leisure time in family activities, most of which have become rare given our current pace of life.

A Brief Interlude

I just returned from a long weekend in New York City. I always look forward to the excitement of visiting the city but not to the crowds, especially on a holiday weekend. I tend to think of New York as generally cold and impersonal with no more human interaction in public than is strictly necessary. For me, it is still worth the visit, despite the mass of humanity.

Several experiences made the crowds disappear if only for a moment. One day, three of us went to lower Manhattan for a show in a theater none of us had ever patronized. Emerging from the subway, we immediately lost our bearings although we did have directions to the theater. We started walking in one random direction to see where it would take us, but did not recognize any of the landmarks we expected.

We encountered a statuesque, gorgeous young woman heading in the opposite direction and asked her if she knew where the Astor Theater was. She stepped aside from her brisk pace and gave us detailed directions to the theater, several blocks from where we stood.

She then resumed walking and disappeared into the crowd. We turned around and started in the right direction. At the next corner, we found her waiting for us, ready with additional guidance should we need it. I was surprised that she would take time from her walk to wait for us.

We found the theater but still had plenty of time before the show. We returned to the previous block where a street festival was in full swing, perused the stands and their wares and chose some food offered by one of the vendors. As we were eating, I noticed a beggar telling everyone he saw that he was hungry but getting no response. I decided it would be a nice gesture to buy him something to eat.

As I pondered this, a policeman appeared on the scene. I imagined that he had been summoned by one of the vendors. He approached the beggar and told him to wait for him at a nearby barricade. He then bought some food and brought it to the beggar, who went on his way. I had never seen a policeman treat a vagrant in this way and I thanked him for caring about the man.

Later, on the subway, we entered an almost full car in lower Manhattan. The subway took on more and more riders as we approached midtown. After a few stops it was downright crowded. I was trying to keep my balance holding onto a pole as three other people were doing at the same time. After one stop, the subway lurched and we all bumped into each other. I thought the girl I was facing would find the bump annoying. Instead she looked at each of us with her charming smile, providing our little group with a moment of delight.

Cultural Values

The trends we considered before the interlude form our cultural pattern. Each society has its own laws, rules and customs which its members are expected to follow. We certainly have a variety of lifestyles within our culture as does every other culture on earth.

Most cultures start with good intentions and strive to meet the needs of at least some of their people, usually the ones with more power. Some of the traditional cultures of the past offered more equality to most if not all their members. In most modern cultures, no matter what their professed values, a few people end up with most of the wealth, some people with next to nothing and the rest somewhere in between.

We can imagine a society in which we all share equally and contribute what we can. Communism professed a belief in such a society but never achieved it in practice. Western cultures, such as our own, value independence and equal opportunity, at least in theory.

Although we have many people in our culture who care about the less fortunate, we still have quite a few who grab what they can and gladly leave everyone else behind to fend for themselves. In the end, the difference in levels of financial prosperity creates its own stress.

Those with power and money fear they will lose what they have. Those less fortunate see the excesses of the wealthy and often end up feeling downtrodden. Perhaps someday we will find a way to combine self determination and caring for each other. It's still a work in progress at best. Sometimes it seems to be moving backwards. In the meantime, our suspicion, distrust and outright hatred of each other keep us at each other's throats and further mired in stress.

What Is Good for Me

Most of us stop to think about this once in a while. You can look at what you want from a selfish point of view without regard for the well being of anyone else on earth. People who take this approach seldom end up happy and often find themselves entangled in their own schemes. They are constantly on guard and looking over their shoulders, fearing attempts at revenge by those whom they have trampled on the way to the top.

You can also look at what is best for you in the context of what others need. Like it or not, you are a social animal. Your best chance of meeting your own needs is in cooperation with others. In some way or another, everything you do affects everyone else and what they do affects you.

You might not realize it at the time, but your transgressions toward others will come back to haunt you eventually. Likewise your kindness toward others will also be repaid, perhaps when you least expect it. Interacting with others in a spirit of friendship and cooperation also lessens stress. Just imagine the difference between how you feel in a room full of close friends compared to one filled with strangers and possible enemies.

The Dream of the Earth

Here is what Thomas Berry had to say in his book, *Dream of the Earth*: "What is needed on our part is the capacity for listening to what the earth is telling us." Before he wrote this book, I had the good fortune to have him as my mentor in a monastery where I lived. I will be forever grateful for his guidance and prudent recommendations.

Some people realize and accept that they are part of the world community. Others think that the only things important in the universe are those within their grasp.

I remember a Dr. Seuss story called *Horton Hears a Who*. The lesson for me was that there are larger and smaller planes of existence than the human one. We just don't pay much attention to them. We gain some perspective on our own level of existence by peering through a microscope or telescope.

Father Augustine Hennessy, whom I mentioned earlier, described marriage as never being static. It is either growing or dying depending on how much care it receives from the spouses involved. I think the same is true of the earth. How we live on our planet helps it to blossom or wilt. Like a plant, the earth flourishes when we take care of it and starts to die when we ignore or abuse it. We can tend it as a beloved garden or hasten its becoming a wasteland.

The earth reacts to stress just like we do. Its equilibrium is thrown off kilter and it becomes unstable. Polluting its atmosphere, oceans and natural habitats makes it harder for the earth's inhabitants to thrive. Being careless with our earth lessens its ability to provide us with an environment supporting life as we know it.

We are beginning to see what it would take to keep our earth healthy and some of the changes which would be required of us. But to do what must be done costs money as well as requiring changes in how we live. We are left with the choice of pillaging our planet or investing in its future for the sake of our descendents.

The more money people have, they more they tend to cling to it, save it for themselves and leave it to their descendents rather than using it to take responsibility for a healthy earth. Of course not all wealthy people are that selfish. No one individual can save or destroy the earth alone. Regardless of our degree of wealth, each of us can contribute to the health of our planet and make it a better place for us all to live. Working together, we can also leave a living legacy for those who follow in our footsteps.

We have choices to make everyday. Some of them affect just our own lives. Some affect a few people around us. Other choices have varying effects on all of us. Sometimes the effects are hard to see. If you throw one little piece of trash on the floor of your house, it might be unsightly, but does not make a great deal of difference to anyone else unless they happen to live with you. If you do it every day, and everyone who enters your house does the same, soon you will have a trash heap rather than a home. The same goes for the earth.

Spirituality of the Future

Many religions and spiritual practices were developed with the goal of bringing people together in peace to seek God together. Unfortunately many religions have also become proprietary. "My religion is the one true one while yours is in error." "Salvation is possible only for those following my religion while all others are excluded from heaven." For centuries we have had a war of religions for ownership of God. See what Karen Armstrong had to say about this in her book, *The Battle for God.*

It sounds strange to even talk about this, yet throughout history much blood has been shed in the name of religion. Various religions fought to destroy or dominate each other in contradiction of the very principles on which they were founded. In recent decades, religions have finally begun taking steps to understand each other and to seek communality rather than competing for souls. This trend may provide incentives to reduce inter-religious conflict and its associated stress in the future.

On a personal level, following the professed goals of most religions might also lead to less stress in your life. Most religions stress simplification of life to what is important. Living your life for a higher purpose than accumulation of wealth and possessions might well offer you the best chance of reducing your own internal stress.

This would work best if everyone on earth did it at the same time. Such a global effort seems unlikely and remote. But, regardless of what others do, you can adopt this approach for yourself. Others seeing your example and how it improves your life might feel an invitation to join you. It's worth a try.

I talked from time to time in this book about Ruiz's books, *The Four Agreements* and *The Fifth Agreement*. I also wrote about the first four agreements in my earlier book, *Commonsense Wisdom for Everyday Life*. I would like to end this book by summarizing what I presented elsewhere about the first four agreements. I think they will give you a head start toward a more peaceful and less stressful life.

Be Impeccable with Your Word

Say what you mean and mean what you say. Moore encourages you to avoid gossip which serves no worthwhile purpose. I have discovered three ways to be impeccable. The first is to be sure that what you say is true. If you can't be sure, don't say it. The second is to be kind in everything you say. It is easy to criticize others to make yourself feel better by comparison. Yet the net result is that the other person feels bad about what you said or becomes angry at you, neither result being good for their or your stress level. The third is to use your words for a good purpose rather than just to hear yourself talk.

Do Not Take Anything Personally

What do you think and how do you feel when someone does something that hurts you? Whether you are assaulted, made fun of, or put down in conversation by someone, it is easy to take it personally. This person does not like you and wants to hurt you. Why else would he or she have done this to you?

Why indeed? Would it surprise you to learn that people do things for their own purposes? Often their reasons have nothing to do with you. What people say and do follows directly from how they think and feel about themselves. They act for their own reasons, hoping to improve their situation. They might think that attacking you will make life better for them somehow.

Do Not Make Assumptions

You just saw one kind of assumption, assuming that another person's actions have something to do with you. If you think about it, you are invited to make assumptions all the time. People might have many different motivations for what they do but they don't announce them to the world. Unless you ask them, you can only guess their reasons.

The most common assumption is that others do what they do for the same reasons you would under similar circumstances. Your assumption might or might not be true. Take time to clarify what others believe and how they feel.

Always Do your Best

Again, we discussed this earlier. This agreement seems difficult to follow until you stop to think about it. Your best effort means what you can do right now in your present circumstances. Your best will vary from day to day and will not be as good under stress as it might be when things are calmer for you. Be sure not to judge yourself too harshly when you are working under adverse circumstances.

What Is Next

My goal in writing this book has not been to provide the last word on stress. I don't have all the answers and don't think anyone else does either. I should mention that the most comprehensive book on Stress I found in my research was Robert Sopolsky's book, *Why Zebras Don't Get Ulcers*.

I have written what I have learned about stress from my personal experience with it and from my work as a psychologist. I hope you will find my comments on stress helpful in keeping you on the path you have set for your life and that they might help you live a little more peacefully. Perhaps our paths will cross one day and we can compare notes.

I have included a list of books I have found useful in my life, especially in understanding stress, how it affects our lives and what we can do about it. I encourage you to explore some of these readings if you want to know more about stress.

Life Lab Lessons

- Find Ways to respect the environment.
- Eat responsibly for your health.
- Reflect on your values to see if they still make sense to you.
- Consider your global family in how you live.
- Try out the four agreements in your daily life.

About the Author

Dr. Langen graduated from the University of Illinois in 1971 with a Ph.D. in Counseling Psychology.

He worked at Temple University Counseling Center offering individual and group therapy for Temple students.

He next worked at De La Salle in Towne, an alternative high school and treatment program for delinquent boys in Philadelphia.

He then moved to Western New York where he worked as Supervising Psychologist at Genesee County Mental Health Services in Batavia, specializing in treatment of teens and alcoholics.

At DePaul Mental Health in Rochester he held the position of Chief Psychologist and Child and Adolescent Team Leader, offering individual, family and group counseling. He also participated in the Child Abuse Treatment Program.

He then entered private practice, offering individual and family therapy with children, teens and adults which he conducted in Williamsville NY and Batavia NY.

He began writing a newsletter for his private practice on commonsense wisdom topics. In 2000, he switched to a biweekly newspaper column at the Daily News in Batavia which he continues to publish. His columns are also published online as **Sliding Otter Newsletter**, available by free subscription at **www.eepurl.com/mSt-P**.

He has published four books. They are all available in eBooks format from Smashwords.com and Amazon Kindle Books. Here is the list:

- *Commonsense Wisdom for Everyday Life,* a collection of reflections on life first published in The Daily News in Batavia.

- *Young Man of the Cloth*, a memoir of his nine years in the Catholic seminary and monastery.

- The *Pastor's Inferno*, a novel about an abusive priest coming to terms with his abuse.

- *Navigating Life: Commonsense Reflections for the Voyage*, a second collection of reflections.

He also maintains a blog, Chats with My Muse, a dialog with his muse, Calliope about the writing process, its challenges and delights available at **www.slidingotter.wordpress.com**.

Personal Note- I wrote this book to share with you what I have learned about stress through my own personal experience and from my years of working with individuals, families and couples. I think the topics we covered can lead to a more peaceful life for you and to a more peaceful world. If you agree and found this book helpful, please consider writing a review on Amazon. You can do so at the Amazon sales page for this book.

Suggested Readings

American Psychiatric Association. *Diagnostic and Statistical Manual of Mental Disorders*, 1994.

Norman Anderson, et al. *Stress in America: Missing the Health Care Connection*. Washington, DC: American Psychological Association, 2013.

Karen Armstrong, *The Battle for God*. NY: Ballantine, 2000.

Melody Beatty. *Codependent No More*. Center City, MN: Hazelden Publishing, 2009.

Melody Beatty. *The Language of Letting Go*. NY: Hay House Publishing, 1990.

Thomas Berry. *The Dream of the Earth*. San Francisco, CA: Sierra Club Books, 1988.

John Bradshaw. *Healing the Shame That Binds You*. Deerfield Beach, FL: Health Communications, Inc., 1988.

Kelly Brownell and Mark Gold. *Food and Addiction. A Comprehensive Handbook*, NY: Oxford University Press, 2012.

Albert Ellis and Robert Harper. *A New Guide to Rational Living*. Chatsworth CA: Wilshire Book Company, 1976.

Bruce Fisher and Robert Alberti. *Rebuilding When Your Relationship Ends*. Atascadero, CA: Impact Publishers, 2000.

Carl Hart and Charles Ksir. *Drugs, Society and Human Behavior*. NY: McGraw Hill, 2012.

Jean Kinney. *Loosening the Grip (Edition 11)*. New York: McGraw Hill, 2014.

Elizabeth Kubler-Ross. *On Death and Dying (Revised edition)*. NY: Scribner, 1997.

Joseph Langen. *Commonsense Wisdom for Everyday Life*. Sliding Otter Publications. Smashwords.com, 2012.

Joseph Langen. *Navigating Life: Reflections for the Voyage*. Sliding Otter Publications, Smashwords.com, 2012.

Joseph Langen. *Young Man of the Cloth*. Sliding Otter Publications, Smashwords.com, 2012.

Elizabeth Lesser. *The New American Spirituality: A Seeker's Guide*. NY: Random House, 1999.

Thomas Moore. *Care of the Soul: A Guide for Cultivating Depth and Sacredness in Everyday Life*. NY: Harper Collins, 1992.

Thomas Moore, *Original Self: Living with Paradox and Originality*. NY: Perennial, 2001.

Don Miguel Ruiz. *The Four Agreements: A Toltec Wisdom Book*. San Rafael, CA: Amber-Allen Publishing, 1997.

Don Miguel Ruiz and Don Jose Ruiz. *The Fifth Agreement: A Toltec Wisdom Book*. San Rafael, CA: Amber-Allen Publishing, 2010.

Robert Sapolsky. *Why Zebras Don't Get Ulcers*. Third Edition. NY: Holt, 2004.

Hans Selye. *The Stress of Life*. NY: McGraw Hill, 1956.

Dr. Seuss. *Horton Hears a Who*. NY: Random House, 1954.

David Snarch. *Passionate Marriage*. NY: W.W. Norton and Company, 1997.

Henry David Thoreau. *Walden*. Radford, VA: Wilder Publications (reprint), 2008

Carla Wills-Brandon. *Learning to Say No: Establishing Healthy Boundaries*. Deerfield Beach, CA: Health Communications, 1990.